THE LEGAL EAGLES GUIDE FOR CHILDREN'S ADVOCACY CENTERS, *PART III*

The Legal Eagles Guide for Children's Advocacy Centers, *Part III*

Soaring for Advocacy and Justice

Andrew H. Agatston

COPYRIGHT © 2012 BY ANDREW H. AGATSTON.

LIBRARY OF CONGRESS CONTROL NUMBER:		2012911581
ISBN:	HARDCOVER	978-1-4771-3482-5
	SOFTCOVER	978-1-4771-3481-8
	EBOOK	978-1-4771-3483-2

All rights reserved. No part of this book may be reproduced or transmitted in any form or by any means, electronic or mechanical, including photocopying, recording, or by any information storage and retrieval system, without permission in writing from the copyright owner.

This book was printed in the United States of America.

To order additional copies of this book, contact:
Xlibris Corporation
1-888-795-4274
www.Xlibris.com
Orders@Xlibris.com
90563

CONTENTS

Foreword 9
Chapter 1   The Trend of Attacking the Forensic Interview 11
Chapter 2   The Forensic Interview Attacks, Part II 14
Chapter 3   The Georgia Supreme Court Changes the Rules 18
Chapter 4   Child Hearsay and Evidence Admissibility Issues 22
Chapter 5   Camreta v. Greene and the Motivations to Sue 25
Chapter 6   Camreta v. Greene and its Potential Impact 28
Chapter 7   Credibility, Veracity, and Bolstering 31
Chapter 8   How To Be A SuperWitness 34
Chapter 9   For Witnesses, It's the Fear of the Unknown 37
Chapter 10 Multiple Relevant Purposes of Documents 41
Chapter 11 Talking About Witness Testimony, and
            Revisiting the SuperWitness 44
Chapter 12 A Top 5 List to Keep the CAC Machine Running Smoothly 47
Chapter 13 The CAC's "Eight Iron" 51
Chapter 14 Are We Up To Task of Our "Teachable Moment" Opportunity? 54
Chapter 15 The Records Request Dilemma—To Give or Not to Give? 56
Chapter 16 Can That Forensic Interview DVD be Released to the Public? 60
Chapter 17 Receiving a Court Order and Reacting 62
Chapter 18 Lawsuits Against CACs? Take action! 66
Chapter 19 Laying the Foundation Before Credibility Attacks at Trial 69
Chapter 20 The "Victim-Witness" Professional: A Case Study in
            Getting Subpoenaed When You Don't Expect It 72

Chapter 21 The Dynamics of the Witness Veracity Attack: One Case Study 76

Chapter 22 Question at Trial: What is the Purpose of Protocols? 80

Chapter 23 Give Circumstantial Evidence the Respect it Deserves! 84

Chapter 24 Discussing Some of the Dynamics that Occur in
Child Custody Cases 87

Chapter 25 Evidence That Appellate Judges Rely Upon 90

Chapter 26 The Substandard Lawyer Performance—And
What You Can Do About It 93

Epilogue and Acknowledgments 97

My admiration for the selfless work of this country's Children's Advocacy Center community continues, and this third Legal Eagles of CACs volume is again dedicated to them, because they make children feel safe in their communities . . .

Foreword

This is the third Legal Eagles book. It all started with the 2009 book, *The Legal Eagles of Children's Advocacy Centers: A Lawyer's Guide to Soaring in the Courtroom* dedicated to advocates for children who were sexually and physically abused. As the number of Legal Eagles grew and expanded to 35 states, the second book *The Legal Eagles of Children's Advocacy Centers: Soaring Confidently in the Courtroom* was written. By that time, we had Legal Eagles receiving articles on the Legal List List Serv in 40 states.

As with the first two books, this book is also a compilation of weekly Legal Letters sent to members of my Legal Eagles List Serv. We are now into our 6th year of the List Serv, covering almost all of our 50 states. But our job is not done—not even close. My vision for all CACs is for all of them to have competent and qualified legal counsel.

Yes, I would like to see my List Serv go out of business!

The support and dedication of CAC professionals over the past six years has been amazing and very humbling. I am grateful for recommendations and feedback from those who do the most important work.

A quick word on this book's content. All three books were compiled after my review of recent Georgia appellate cases. Every state has the ability through its legislature to enact its own statues (or laws), and every state has its own appellate courts that interpret its own state statutes. The fact patterns in this book will likely mirror those that occur in your state; however, the manner in which your legislature and your courts interpret the fact patterns may and will differ. Make sure that you have a competent and qualified attorney who can work for your CAC and interpret the fact patterns, and then research the case law and the statues that apply to your center and your state. This book is not designed to provide your CAC (or you) with legal advice.

If you are a professional affiliated with a CAC who would like to join our humble and growing List Serv, please let me know. I can be reached through my website, www.AgatstonLaw.com. All the best to all of you!

—Andrew Agatston, 2012

Chapter One

The Trend of Attacking the Forensic Interview

Legal Eagles—The trend in the appellate cases continues. Another child molestation conviction appealed, in part, because the Defendant blamed the defense lawyer for not offering expert testimony to rebut the prosecution witnesses who testified about the forensic interview of the child and the forensic interviewing process.

If there is one word that is increasingly used in defendant appeals involving child molestation cases, at least the ones I'm reading week in and week out, it is: Suggestibility. Is there any other issue out there related to appeals of convictions that people are seeing that tops this one? If so, please let me know.

Know about the topic. Read about it. Know the principles, primarily expressed by Ceci & Bruck. And also know that there have been papers written in response to Ceci & Bruck and other suggestibility researchers, such as those written by Thomas Lyon. There have also been studies addressing the susceptibility of children to suggestibility conducted by researchers that actually involve children who have alleged abuse, as opposed to many of the studies cited by suggestibility researchers that do not involve such children. It is important to learn from all of them, and important not to discount any of them.

There is much more to this topic, and it is beyond debate that those whose work involves encountering children who have alleged abuse must be well versed in the theory and science of suggestibility, from all perspectives. If you are not, then the new chapter should begin today.

For forensic interviewers, the importance of continued training, reading, reviewing, etc., cannot be overstated. It would not be an uncommon set of questions by an attorney to ask about the various suggestibility studies that are often cited in the research, and then compare and contrast the findings with the forensic interview process that occurred in the particular case before the jury.

In today's case, however, suggestibility was not debated at trial, because the defense lawyer decided not to call an expert to rebut the forensic interviewer's techniques.

Facts: The Defendant was convicted of two counts of child molestation involving his stepdaughter. A forensic interview was completed, where she disclosed abuse, including that the Defendant would put ointment on her genitals and buttocks after her evening showers. The victim stated that after the second or third time, the Defendant told her not to tell, and threatened her with spankings if she ever told anyone of the encounters.

Prior to arrest, the Defendant agreed to talk to the detective. At first he denied ever touching the victim's genitals or buttocks, but later admitted that he once put medicine on her buttocks and genitals to treat redness and irritation. He also said he examined her genitals after she dried herself too hard after a bath and showed him that her vagina was red.

Result: Conviction affirmed.

The Defendant argued on appeal that he was denied effective assistance of counsel at trial because his lawyer did not call an expert witness who had been retained by the defense and was prepared to testify that the State had used improper forensic interviewing techniques in the case.

The expert who was retained testified at the Defendant's Motion for New Trial hearing about her review of the evidence in the case, including the child interviews, which "she thought were unreasonably suggestive and conducted improperly." She discussed with the defense lawyer that she had "serious concerns" about the interviewing techniques used. She said she was under subpoena, and was prepared to testify.

She was asked whether she ever told the defense lawyer that her testimony about the interviewing techniques would be unfavorable to the defense.

She responded: "Well, it depends on what you mean by not favorable for the defense . . . [i]n looking at all the data, everything that I'm provided in a case, I will always tell an attorney these are the things that support the allegations, these are the things that don't support it. So there possibly would be asked questions that might not support his questioning."

She also described facts that supported the State. And she mentioned that "she had an important annual family trip planned that she 'really wanted to go on,'" but she did not recall telling the defense lawyer that she would not be available to testify.

Unfortunately, there was nothing in the appellate opinion that indicated what the expert believed was "suggestible" questioning during the forensic interview.

However, the defense attorney, who testified at the Motion for New Trial hearing, indicated that he believed the expert was backing down from her opinion at the time of the trial, and that a California trip may have been the reason. "Seemed like what she was saying then was not quite the same thing that was helpful. And I got the idea she just didn't want to be a witness and probably would not make a good one with it like that."

But what if there were fireworks at trial? What are some of the critiques? Can you name them, based upon some suggestibility articles that defense lawyers might use to critique a forensic interviewer?

Here are a few, according to articles on suggestibility that I have read and which you can research on your own (and there are many others):

1. Interview bias—the interviewer's belief of an event that can influence the accuracy of the children's answers.
2. Specific open-ended questions. This occurs when the subject perpetrator's name is included in the open-ended question: "Tell me what happened with Fred."
3. Forced choice questions: An example would be, "Were you touched under the clothes or over the clothes?"
4. Repeated specific question. An example would be (repeatedly), "Did he touch you under the clothes?"
5. Repeated misinformation. Self-explanatory.
6. Questions were asked in an emotional atmosphere.
7. Stereotype induction. This is where the interviewer talks about how bad the perpetrator is. "He's a bad man who did bad things to other kids. Now, did the bad man do anything to you?"
8. Subtle influences—parents' subtle influences that may occur either before your interaction with the child or after your interaction with the child. When they are followed up by intense questions stating that something happened, the theory is that it can lead to a sexual abuse interpretation in the child.

I want to stress again that there are many, many papers written that are accessible and that make important and well-cited responses to the suggestibility research used by the defense. The National CAC is a great resource to locate the research.

It's a big topic that is getting bigger. If you survey the appellate cases, the appeals are zeroing in on suggestibility.

Chapter Two

The Forensic Interview Attacks, Part II

Legal Eagles—I'm still on an "attack the forensic interview analysis" tear.

For those of you who are not forensic interviewers, this involves you, too. For example, one of the case strategies involves examining anyone who speaks to the child at any time after the child's initial outcry to determine whether their discussion with the child could have "tainted" the ultimate disclosure during the forensic interview, if there was one. It can also involve therapists who provide therapy to a child after disclosure, and who report either additional details of the initial disclosure, or new details altogether.

This case is from November 2009, and while the case facts are unusual, the end points that I want to make are not.

Facts: The Defendant was convicted of first degree cruelty to children and aggravated battery for removing his daughter's clitoris. When the victim was two years old, the Defendant moved out of the house. Several months later, he called the victim's mother (his ex-wife at the time of trial) and wanted to pick up their daughter, but she refused. The mother explained that because the Defendant was born in Ethiopia and "because of his culture," she believed that he wanted to have their daughter circumcised. As such, she refused to allow him to pick up their daughter. He answered, "How do you know I haven't already done it?" and added, "What's done is done."

That prompted the mother to take her daughter to medical exams, which confirmed that the child's clitoris had been removed. The child at the time was 3 years old.

Her mother took her to a psychotherapist, who testified at trial. He was tendered as an expert in child trauma and child memory, as well as forensic interviewing and evaluating.

The Court opinion stated that "During a forensic interview in March 2003, the child disclosed that her father had cut her 'lun-lun,' a word the child used to refer to her private area."

The expert then testified that it was possible for the then 3-year-old to have an accurate memory of something that had been done to her more than a year earlier, which was the time-frame alleged at trial. According to the Court of Appeals opinion, the expert testified that "[C]hildren about two years old 'can remember impactful episodes more acutely than they can remember ordinary episodes.'"

Finally, the expert testified that during the next two years of therapy, the child never recanted her disclosure.

At trial, the victim (who was then 7 years old) testified that "[My father] cut my private part."

The defense theory was that the Defendant didn't do it; instead, the victim's maternal grandmother did. The jury convicted the Defendant. On appeal, he argued that the trial court was in error for rejecting his claim of ineffective assistance of counsel.

Remember that such claim means that the Defendant believes that his trial counsel's performance at trial was not only deficient, but that the alleged deficient performance was prejudicial to his defense.

Result: Conviction affirmed.

Topics for you to consider: One of Defendant's complaints on appeal was that the defense lawyer should not have called a clinical psychologist who testified as a defense expert, because the lawyer failed to adequately investigate the psychologist's background. More on that later.

First, let's review what the defense psychologist testified about, and why he was called. He was called to attempt to discredit what had been presented to the jury by the State about the child's memory. In this regard, the Court accepted the psychologist as an expert in (1) child psychology; (2) forensic interviewing of children; (3) memory recall in children; (4) false memories; and (5) false beliefs.

As to the forensic interview, the Court of Appeals highlighted two criticisms advanced by the defense expert: (1) interviewer bias, and (2) suggestive comments and questioning.

Specifically, according to the Court of Appeals the defense expert testified that the forensic interviewer displayed bias against the father and in favor of the mother in his questioning, and "had made impermissible suggestions to the child that her father had hurt her. In addition, the expert cited areas that he claimed the interviewer should have explored with the child, given her responses and emotional reactions during the interview."

As to a child's memory, the defense expert stated that children such as the victim, at the age she was interviewed, have "very unreliable, very inconsistent" memories. They hear what adult authority figures say, and this "becomes their memory." According to the Court of Appeals opinion, he testified that "there appeared to a great possibility that the child's allegations made during the forensic interview had been contaminated by improper influences, including 'something that was told to her prior to the interview,' as well as 'leading questions and words that were fed her during the forensic interview.'"

There was no discussion in the Court of Appeals opinion about how the State addressed these opinions of the defense expert. Suffice it to say that there are highly credible opposing views and theories to the defense expert's opinions.

But intertwined with the defense expert's opinions was the defense expert's professional background, which was striking enough to lead the Defendant to claim that his lawyer should not have called the expert as a witness in the first place. Specifically, the psychologist had been suspended from his profession, and also had written a book titled, "Screw Your Spouse, Win the Kids, and Make Money Doing It."

As to the suspension, the expert testified that he had once been ordered to suspend giving testimony in child custody cases, but that the order had been subsequently vacated. As to the book title, he testified that it was "satirical" and "a parody" of "the way the system works right now, how you can help plant false accusations and allegations." He said the book dealt with "suggestibility and describes the strategies of winning children in custody battles by setting of false memories and suggestibility."

An expert witness's background including the pitfalls of having, shall we say, a checkered resume can be a topic of a Legal Letter all on its own. But in short, we know that a witness's credibility, in every regard, is the key to being a SuperWitness.

But let's take the variable of this particular defense expert, being so full of himself, out of the equation, and instead make him a professor at a prestigious university, or a psychologist affiliated with a prestigious healthcare organization.

Now we get to the heart of the matter, with no unnecessary credibility distractions. Now, instead of dealing with a self-inflicted defense mistake that likely flattened the expert's effectiveness, you're having to deal with impeccable expert credentials and professional theories that have been widely peer reviewed, and endorsed in many quarters.

The answer? Whenever you hear, or read, or listen to these theories that are now routinely discussed in child molestation matters, you <u>must</u> find the reputable articles that describe them, and then find the articles that offer both critical evaluations of them and opposing viewpoints.

Just in this Legal Letter, we mentioned "interview bias," "false memory," "child memory," "suggestibility," "recant," and "false belief." My one lawyer viewpoint is that when someone affiliated with a CAC sees a term of art, locate the journal articles, the research and studies that relate to the topic and <u>read</u> them. Additionally, when you see terms such as "interview bias," "suggestibility," etc., then you know the topic also includes, generally, how children disclose, if they in fact do disclose. There are journal articles and frankly books on this topic.

Consider having a person at the CAC responsible for creating the library for everyone at the Center. Then make the results in your Center's library <u>**a** required reading material</u> for everyone at the Center who interacts with children and non-offending caregivers. If you want to go to the next level, which is a very good place to be, then have regular staff meetings to discuss the various journal topics, so that everyone has a firm understanding about what this literature, which can be convoluted and complex, means.

This information is easily found. One place to start is the CALiO library on the National Children's Advocacy Center website, www.nationalcac.org. It is my understanding that it is the largest online child abuse library in the U.S., with the most such resources, anywhere. Information about the requirements for accessing CALiO by CACs can be obtained by contacting the National CAC in Huntsville, Alabama.

I believe over the last several chapters I've made my position clear that the criminal defense is becoming more adept at understanding CACs, understanding the many variables that go into interviewing children, and finally understanding that there is research on the topics that the defense can attempt to use to defend their clients. Without knowing this research, and knowing the abundant research that credibly and critically analyzes the research that the defense champions use, you're going to Court lacking a very important tool for your toolbox.

Chapter Three

The Georgia Supreme Court Changes the Rules

<u>Case:</u> Hatley v. State, Georgia Supreme Court, Case No.: S11A1617, (Decided February 6, 2012).

<u>Facts:</u> The Defendant was convicted of aggravated child molestation, aggravated sodomy and two counts of sexual battery. On appeal, he urged the Supreme Court to reverse his convictions, arguing that Georgia's "Child Hearsay Statute" was unconstitutional because it violates the Confrontation Clause.

This Georgia Supreme Court opinion followed. And the Georgia Supreme Court issued new rules in Georgia, in light of the landmark U.S. Supreme Court case *Crawford v. Washington*. We have previously written on the *Crawford* case. We also have written extensively on child hearsay and its interplay with forensic interviews.

This case changes certain procedures in child molestation cases in Georgia, e.g., the pretrial procedures necessary to introduce a victim's "testimonial" child hearsay statements contained in forensic interviews. It is important to know how the *Crawford case* affects your state's rules.

First, the Georgia Supreme Court's holding or the "rule of the case" in *Hatley* is that Georgia's Child Hearsay Statute does not, as analyzed in previous Georgia appellate cases, comport with the requirements of the Confrontation Clause.

To understand, let's refresh ourselves on definitions. Georgia's Child Hearsay Statute (the lawyer of your CAC's choice can research your state's rules, including whether child hearsay is even available) is as follows:

> A statement made by a child under the age of 14 years describing any act of sexual contact or physical abuse performed with or on the child by another or performed with or on another in the presence of the child is admissible in evidence by the testimony of the person or persons to whom made if the child <u>is available to testify in the proceedings</u> and the court finds that the circumstances of the statement provide sufficient indicia or reliability.

Child hearsay involves out-of-court statements by the child that cannot be cross-examined. These statements are often brought into evidence through, for example, a parent who learns of the abuse through the child's disclosure. A forensic interview also involves a child's out-of-court statements and, alone, the defense cannot cross-examine the child's statements.

This leads to the Confrontation Clause. The Sixth Amendment Confrontation Clause promises criminal defendants in federal criminal trials or state criminal trials that "in all criminal prosecutions, the accused shall enjoy the right . . . to be confronted with the witnesses against him." Face and cross.

Recall that *Crawford* in 2004 announced a brand new approach to applying the Confrontation Clause to criminal cases. *Crawford* teaches that "testimonial statements" will be excluded from evidence unless the accused has the opportunity to cross-examine the person making the statement. "Non-testimonial" statements will not be excluded.

So we have to refresh ourselves on the "testimonial" v. "nontestimonial" distinction. Stick with me, Legal Eagles!!!

A U.S. Supreme Court case, subsequent to *Crawford*, defined these terms as follows (in *Davis v. Washington*):

> Statements are nontestimonial when made in the course of police interrogation under circumstances objectively indicating that the primary purpose of the interrogation is to enable police assistance to meet on ongoing emergency. Statements are testimonial when the circumstances objectively indicate that there is no such ongoing emergency, and the primary purpose of the interrogation is to establish or prove past events potentially relevant to later criminal prosecution.

With these definitions in tact, how would you categorize 911 calls? In the initial stages, I believe it is very safe to say they are nontestimonial, designed to assist the police to respond to an emergency. But careful, they just might change over to testimonial if the caller's primary purpose shifts to providing facts to prove past events.

Whew!

The point is that the Courts will look closely at the content as well as the context of the statement in order to glean the purpose of the statement.

With that as background, let's turn to the Georgia Supreme Court decision in *Hatley*.

There were a series of three child hearsay statements analyzed by the Georgia Supreme Court: the child's disclosure to her mother; the police interview of the child at the scene on the same day (at a hotel); and the forensic interview that was conducted "a few weeks later."

(Side note: A few weeks later? There was no detail in the opinion about why the forensic interview did not occur for "a few weeks.")

At trial, the trial court allowed the child's mother, the police officers, and the forensic interviewer to testify about what the victim told them. The victim was in the courthouse and available to testify, but she was not called as a witness by the prosecution.

The Defendant argued on appeal that the trial court erred (1) in failing to declare Georgia's Child Hearsay Statute unconstitutional; (2) in failing to require that the State present the victim as a witness; and (3) in permitting the hearsay statements made by the victim and her mother to the police and the forensic interviewer in violation of the Confrontation Clause.

As stated earlier, the Georgia Supreme Court determined that Georgia's Child Hearsay statute, as analyzed in prior Georgia cases, did not comport with the requirements of the Confrontation Clause, and therefore overruled all prior Georgia cases contrary to its current opinion.

It further decided, however, that Georgia's Child Hearsay Statute could satisfy the requirements of the Confrontation Clause by means of a new pretrial notice requirement it announced in its brand-new decision.

Are you still with me?

Accordingly, the Georgia Supreme Court announced a new rule about how it would interpret the Child Hearsay Statute, placing requirements on the State.

The prosecution is required to "notify the defendant within a reasonable period of time prior to trial of its intent to use a child victim's hearsay statements and to give the defendant an opportunity to raise a Confrontation Clause objection. If the defendant objects, and the State wishes to introduce the hearsay statements [pursuant to the Child Hearsay Statute], the State must present the child witness at trial; if the defendant does not object, the State can introduce the child victim's hearsay statements subject to the trial court's determination that the circumstances of the statements provide sufficient indicia of reliability."

From now forward in Georgia if the State seeks to introduce "testimonial" child hearsay, so long as the Defendant objects on Confrontation Clause grounds to such child hearsay being introduced, the child-victim will be called to the stand to testify. Certainly, the child has always been routinely called to testify, but not always, and not in all jurisdictions.

(For those latter jurisdictions, it is critical now that forensic interviewers do not tell the non-offending caregiver that their child will not have to testify at trial if she undergoes an F.I.)

One more point just to drive home the point on the testimonial v. non-testimonial issue. In Georgia, as explicitly stated in the *Hatley* decision, a forensic interview involves testimonial statements, no ifs, ands, or buts. There was no analysis by the Georgia Supreme Court on this point, and frankly I think there should have been. But it's over now. As the Court succinctly stated: "With these cases in mind, we conclude that (the victim's) statements to her mother were nontestimonial, whereas (the victim's) statement to the forensic interviewer, made several weeks after the crimes, was testimonial."

Chapter Four

Child Hearsay and Evidence Admissibility Issues

<u>Case</u>: State v. Stahlnecker, South Carolina Supreme Court., Case No.: 386 S.C. 609 (2010).

<u>Facts</u>: The Defendant lived with his wife and their 2-year-old daughter, as well as his wife's 5-year-old son and her 7-year-old daughter (the victim).

One day the victim was alone with the Defendant, and she testified that on that day the Defendant sexually abused her.

Her mother testified that when she returned home on that day, she saw that the victim had different clothes on than before. The mother testified that she told her daughter to change her clothes, and later the mother checked on the daughter in the daughter's bedroom.

When the mother went into her daughter's bedroom, her daughter was in the fetal position, and said that she wanted to go to bed. When her mother helped her change into her pajamas, her mother noticed that her daughter's panties were wet and a hair was stuck to her daughter's "private area." When asked whether she had been touched by Defendant, her daughter nodded her head yes and began crying.

As with so many child molestation trials, there were child hearsay issues throughout today's case.

And as we know from these cases, there is a number of ways that the hearsay statements of the child-victim are litigated at the trial and reviewed on the appeal after the Defendant's conviction.

In today's case, there was another notable occurrence that we will discuss.

When the victim was taken to the hospital after her outcry, a sex crimes investigator interviewed the victim. The interview was not recorded because it was late at night and the hospital did not have the recording equipment in the room. The investigator testified that she did not conduct a second interview because she obtained a very clear disclosure and she did not want the victim to undergo a second interview. The investigator also testified that this was an emergency-type interview, and she testified about the direct statements that she received from the victim.

Before we dive into the applicable South Carolina statute, we must remember that there have been big changes in the law in many states regarding child hearsay. As a general refresher (since each state will have its own definition) child hearsay for our purposes involves statements made by a child victim (who is under a specific age-14 in Georgia, 12 in S.C., e.g.) to another about a criminal sexual abuse event that happened to him or her. Once that occurs, and as the case proceeds to trial, the factual, procedural, and legal battles regarding whether such child hearsay can be introduced into evidence begin.

But as we've seen in the Legal Letter recently, there are cases that have reined in the ability of prosecutors to use child hearsay due to concerns related to a Defendant's constitutional right of confrontation. For a discussion, please refer to the United States Supreme Court case, *Crawford v. Washington*, 541 U.S. 36 (2004), and its discussion of testimonial v. non-testimonial hearsay.

As we've discussed repeatedly, the harm of hearsay is that it cannot be cross-examined, and therefore tested in court by the opponent of the statement. Thus, the exceptions to hearsay that allow the statement to be introduced in court (realizing the cross examination concern) focus on whether the hearsay statement was reliable and trustworthy, among other factors.

In South Carolina, in cases involving child sexual abuse, a key statute is S.C. Ann. § 17-23-175, which allows the introduction of the forensic interview of a child if certain requirements are met. Thus, one of the issues on appeal in today's case was whether the trial court erred by allowing an unrecorded out-of-court statement of the victim to the investigator to be introduced into evidence under S.C. Ann. § 17-23-175.

Before analyzing this, please realize that each state can and will have different statutory requirements related to these out-of-court statements that appear in forensic interviews. The key is to understand your state's rules through the assistance of a competent and qualified attorney of your CAC's choosing.

In South Carolina, the aforementioned statute, § 17-23-175, must be reviewed, and it relates to out-of-court statements made by children under 12 years old. The S.C. rules of the road, as set out in the statute, are that the out-of-court statement is admissible if: (1) the child's statement was made in response to questioning conducted in an investigative interview of the child; (2) an audio and visual recording of the statement is preserved *[subject to an important exception, to be discussed below]*; (3) the child testifies at the proceeding and is subject to cross-examination on the elements of the criminal offense and the making of the out-of-court statement; and (4) the trial court, in a hearing conducted outside of the presence of the jury, finds that the circumstances surrounding the making of the statement "provides particularized guarantees of trustworthiness."

But recall in this case that the child's statement was not recorded. The South Carolina statute addresses that potential as well, and the South Carolina Supreme Court in today's case analyzed the facts of the case in light of the § 17-23-175 requirements. It found that the trial court did not err in allowing the investigator to testify as to what the child told her because the Supreme Court found that the investigator's explanation for having no equipment, when combined with the indicators of trustworthiness, was satisfactory.

The critical importance of a CAC obtaining qualified legal counsel to advise on CAC needs, the topic of standards for forensic interviews was raised. That is, the National Children's Alliance, and likely your state, has a forensic interview standard that includes that such interviews must be done in a manner that is "legally sound."

What is "legally sound?" The oft-repeated answers go to the *technical* aspect of forensic interviewers, i.e., don't be suggestive, be wary of leading questions, etc.

This can certainly trigger legal concerns related to the admissibility of expert testimony. However, I have other concerns triggered by the "legally sound" standard, and these can be overlooked without legal counsel.

If the standard is going to include a "legally sound" component, then a CAC needs to make sure it has a lawyer to guide them in the "legally sound" analysis. For example, with the South Carolina statute, a lawyer for a South Carolina CAC would scour the words in § 17-23-175, and find the legal requirements necessary for a forensic interview of a child under age 12 to be admitted as part of the state's child hearsay statute. Reading the statute, I would be interested in such terms as "internal coherence" and "detailed account" among others. I would then review the South Carolina case law to determine how the courts have analyzed these and other descriptive terms in prior cases involving trial molestation trials. From there, the CAC lawyer can meet with interviewers and other CAC staff to advise on the law.

There is more to this, and there is more to the term "legally sound," but the launch point is that a standard with this term requires a legal analysis.

Chapter Five

Camreta v. Greene and the Motivations to Sue

Case: Camreta v. Greene, Supreme Court of U.S., (Decided May 26, 2011)

Facts: This case originated in Oregon. It involved a CPS worker, accompanied by a deputy sheriff, who interviewed a 9-year-old girl (S.G.) in her school regarding allegations that her father abused her.

Among other things, the 9th Circuit Court of Appeals held that the these two state officials violated the Constitution by failing to obtain a warrant or court order to conduct the interview, which was done absent "exigent" circumstances or parental consent.

This will be the first in a series of Legal Letters on this case, which sent shivers through children's advocacy circles across the U.S. This Legal Letter discusses my thoughts on the motivations for lawsuit, generally.

Ultimately, the U.S. Supreme Court vacated the 9th Circuit's order regarding the interview issue. In the next chapter, I'll discuss that part of the decision, and what it might mean. What is it that motivates people to file lawsuits? This has particular meaning to me, because as a plaintiff's lawyer, I represent people in civil cases who have been victims of crime. I also wear a lawyer hat advising CACs on various legal matters. Invariably, one issue that comes up is the likelihood that CAC professionals will face civil lawsuits for actions or events arising out of their professional activities.

The first point to discuss is the motivation for filing lawsuits. And immediately we need to discount and dismiss stereotypical answers that conclude the motivations are "greed" or "money" or "jackpot justice." Because those motivations invariably lead to losing lawsuits for plaintiffs, and they create very defensible strategies for civil defendants.

Good plaintiff cases revolve around motivations of "righting a wrong," "ensuring wrongful conduct does not happen to others," and "holding wrongdoers accountable."

As a point of departure, let's review the written arguments made by the parties to the Supreme Court in the Camreta case. There are two sides of a coin, and first, we'll review the facts of the case as set out by the CPS worker and the deputy sheriff, Camreta and Alford:

The following Monday, Camreta and Deputy Sheriff Alford went to S.G.'s public school to interview her. Camreta chose to interview her at her school because schools are "a place where children feel safe" and because doing so would allow him "'to conduct the interview away from the potential influence of suspects, including parents.'" According to Camreta, "'[i]nterviews of this nature, on school premises, are a regular part of [child-protective services] practice and are consistent with DHS rules and training.'" DHS did not inform S.G.'s mother, Sarah, about the interview. Neither Camreta nor Alford obtained a warrant or other court order before the interview.

When Camreta and Alford arrived at S.G.'s school, Camreta told school officials that he and Alford wanted to interview S.G. and he requested use of a private office. Terry Friesen, a school counselor, went to S.G.'s classroom and told her that someone was there to talk with her. Friesen took S.G. to the room where Camreta and Alford were waiting, and then left. According to S.G., Camreta interviewed S.G. for two hours in Alford's presence, although Alford did not ask any questions during the interview. Alford was in uniform and had a visible firearm. The interview was not recorded.

Reading that passage, generally, one could understandably reach the conclusion that the interview was appropriate and proper, and that Camreta and Alford were simultaneously doing their job while protecting the well-being of the child.

But that is the case through the eyes of the Camreta camp. It doesn't come close to measuring the motivations for S.G.'s lawsuit.

It is time to look at the facts through the plaintiff's eyes.

On February 24, 2003, at about 1:00 p.m., a uniformed deputy sheriff with a gun visible in his holster (petitioner James Alford), and an Oregon Department of Human Services ("DHS") investigator (petitioner Bob Camreta) appeared at the Bend elementary school that nine-year-old S.G. attended. The sheriff and investigator directed school staff to remove the girl from her class and bring her to an empty conference room near the principal's office. The school employee left S.G. alone, behind closed doors, with the two male strangers. Alford and Camreta did not identify themselves to S.G. No one explained to her why she was there and she was "too scared to ask [Camreta] any questions." Throughout the two-hour interrogation that ensued, S.G. was too frightened even to ask for a glass of water, much less to tell petitioners that she felt sick.

Although Camreta had learned of the allegations regarding S.G. three or four days earlier, and the police investigation had been pending for two weeks, neither Camreta nor Alford spoke to S.G.'s mother, Sarah Greene, before interrogating S.G., so they did not have her consent to the interview. Camreta and Alford also did not know that S.G. suffered from significant developmental delays, particularly in spoken language, verbal reasoning ability, and overall reasoning. She was eligible for special educational services because of the "communication disorder."

Camreta interrogated S.G. while Alford silently observed. When Camreta asked S.G. if her father touched her "all over [her] body," she said "yes," referring to affectionate hugs, kisses, and piggy-back rides. Camreta then asked "over and over again" if "some of those were bad touches." Over and over again, S.G. said "no." In response to the frightened nine-year-old's repeated and clear denials of abuse, Camreta "would say, 'No that's not it,' and then ask me [S.G.] the same question again."

"For over an hour," Camreta repeated "the same questions, just in different ways . . ." In the process, he educated S.G. about child sexual abuse; S.G. had been unfamiliar with the topic.

S.G. denied all allegations of abuse for almost two hours.

S.G. was so upset by the coercive interrogation that she vomited five times that night after returning home. She could not eat dinner or even drink Gatorade.

Putting aside the accuracy of these statements, as we are not privy to the record (and also the Plaintiff's allegations were hotly disputed), it is easy to see that, now, we have some of motivations for the lawsuit. We have a plaintiff who has alleged heavy-handed tactics from the state; tactics that allegedly created suggestive responses in a 9-year-old child; and a failure to include S.G.'s mother in the process.

By trying to see the lawsuit through the eyes of the opposing side, we can begin to understand facts and circumstances that motivate plaintiffs to file lawsuits. That, in turn, provides CACs and their professionals a window to look through—and which can lead CAC professionals away from unproductive, ineffective or questionable acts or activities that can be later used as a hook to hang a legal theory in a lawsuit.

Chapter Six

Camreta v. Greene and its Potential Impact

Case: Camreta v. Greene, Supreme Court of U.S., (Decided May 26, 2011)

Facts: We have reviewed and analyzed Camreta v. Greene, the case that originated in Oregon, several times. It involved a CPS worker, accompanied by a deputy sheriff, who interviewed a 9-year-old girl (S.G.) in her school regarding allegations that her father abused her.

Among other things, the 9th Circuit Court of Appeals held that the these two state officials violated the Constitution by failing to obtain a warrant or court order to conduct the interview, which was done absent "exigent" circumstances or parental consent.

The U.S. Supreme Court vacated the 9th Circuit's order regarding the interview issue. The crux of the opinion was on legal issues not related to child sexual abuse investigations. But a light has certainly been shined on the issue of parental consent for a F.I.

The lawsuits that have better potential for success, which don't revolve around "greed" or "money" or "jackpot justice," but "righting a wrong," "ensuring wrongful conduct does not happen to others," and "holding wrongdoers accountable."

The plaintiffs in *Camreta* believed that they had such a case, and as it traveled in the federal court system up to the Ninth Circuit Court of Appeals, they continued to have a fighting chance.

Recall that the facts surrounding the in-school interview of the young child alleged to have been abused, issues, as expressed from the standpoint of the Plaintiff's brief to the U.S. Supreme Court, were as follows:

> The following Monday, Camreta and Deputy Sheriff Alford went to S.G.'s public school to interview her. Camreta chose to interview her at her school because schools are "a place where children feel safe" and because doing so would allow him "'to conduct the interview away from the potential influence of suspects, including parents.'" According to Camreta, "'[i]nterviews of this nature, on school premises, are a regular part of [child-protective services] practice and are consistent with DHS rules and training.'" DHS did not

inform S.G.'s mother, Sarah, about the interview. Neither Camreta nor Alford obtained a warrant or other court order before the interview.

When Camreta and Alford arrived at S.G.'s school, Camreta told school officials that he and Alford wanted to interview S.G. and he requested use of a private office. Terry Friesen, a school counselor, went to S.G.'s classroom and told her that someone was there to talk with her. Friesen took S.G. to the room where Camreta and Alford were waiting, and then left. According to S.G., Camreta interviewed S.G. for two hours in Alford's presence, although Alford did not ask any questions during the interview. Alford was in uniform and had a visible firearm. The interview was not recorded.

Recall that the Ninth Circuit Court of Appeals decided that, as the plaintiffs had argued, the government officials (the CPS worker and the law enforcement officer) had violated the U.S. Constitution by failing to obtain a warrant or parental consent of the child to conduct the interview. The Ninth Circuit also decided, however, that Camreta and Greene were entitled to "qualified immunity," and thus they could not be held liable for the constitutional violation.

Thus, the case arrived in the U.S. Supreme Court under unique circumstances: although Camreta and Greene could not be held liable due to qualified immunity, they asked the U.S. Supreme Court to review and clarify the underlying Fourth Amendment (search and seizure) issue, to in fact determine whether their interview was violative of the Constitution.

Confusing? Yes. But once the U.S. Supreme Court began oral argument on the matter, it became apparent that it was not going to reach the Fourth Amendment issue. And that is what happened. The U.S. Supreme Court declined to rule on the underlying Fourth Amendment question because it found that the case was "moot." "Moot" means that it was decided there was no longer a controversy to decide.

Why? The interview of the child in question occurred nine years ago, she is now a high school graduate, and she lives in another state. Therefore, there is "not the slightest possibility of [her] being seized in a school in the Ninth Circuit's jurisdiction as part of a child abuse investigation." That is "moot."

So if the U.S. Supreme Court didn't decide the Fourth Amendment issue related to the interview of the child by a CPS worker and by law enforcement in a school, how should protocols and procedures in the same or similar circumstances be affected in the future?

Part of the answer to that question involves an mind-numbing analysis of constitutional law. That is, it involves a discussion of whether the constitutional right that is being claimed by the Plaintiff is "clearly established" in law.

To determine whether it is "clearly established," generally, the governmental actors (in this case the CPS worker and the deputy) have to be on notice that their actions violated the constitutional rights of the Plaintiff. This notice is established by prior appellate opinions that have settled the asserted constitutional right, so that governmental officials are given "fair notice" of the right.

This is confusing, even to lawyers. To illustrate: if I suffer damage due to the actions of a governmental actor, such as a CPS worker, then I might want to bring a lawsuit against that person for the violation of my constitutional rights. That is what happened in the Camreta case.

In order for me to prevail, the constitutional right that I assert was violated has to be 1) clearly established and 2) the governmental actor had to be on "fair notice" that his actions that I allege violated by constitutional rights were "clearly established," as evidence by a prior reported case.

So the question arises: Can the Ninth Circuit's opinion be used as "fair notice" to show that such an interview as occurred in Camreta was a "clearly established" constitutional violation? It was reported in a published opinion, but the U.S. Supreme Court vacated the crux of its decision.

Let's look at what happened in the in Oregon after the Ninth Circuit's Camreta decision.

The Ninth Circuit told government officials to follow specific standards to govern all in-school interviews of suspected child abuse victims. The Ninth Circuit instructed government officials to follow those standards going forward, and "cease operating on the assumption" that warrantless interviews are permitted.

The question for Oregon is whether these instructions must be followed after the Supreme Court's opinion. It is something that Oregon lawyers will have to determine, as well as lawyers in other jurisdictions across the U.S.

Recall that the U.S. Supreme Court didn't answer the question because the case was moot. But another such case will surely come along, and the question is whether officials who interview children in this situation will decide to follow dictates similar to those set forth by the Ninth Circuit.

Chapter Seven

Credibility, Veracity, and Bolstering

<u>Case:</u> Damerow v. State, Georgia Court of Appeals, Case No. A11A0338, (Decided July 6, 2011).

<u>Facts:</u> The Defendant was convicted of child molestation of his stepdaughter. When the victim was 13 years old, the Defendant began grabbing her buttocks and forcing her to kiss him. The victim disclosed the incidents to her mother, who removed the Defendant from the home and obtained a divorce.

However, the next year, the mother allowed the Defendant to move back into the home, and the molestation continued and escalated. The victim testified that the Defendant molested her nightly, and told her that he would kill her and her family if she told anyone.

Ultimately, the victim disclosed the abuse to a friend whose father was a police officer. An investigation began, and included a forensic interview. Additionally, the victim obtained counseling, and at trial the counselor testified.

The Defendant focused on credibility issues, and issues of alleged bolstering by the State's witnesses on appeal. It can be said with confidence that credibility and veracity are the Twin Peaks of effective witnesses. There is no wonder why so many appeals focus on witnesses' credibility and veracity, and related facts from the case that a convicted Defendant believes caused prejudice during his trial.

One of those oft-appealed complaints focuses on improper "bolstering" testimony by a witness in favor of the alleged victim. We have reviewed many cases in the past on this topic, and today's case follows. It is critically important to understand the bright line rule on bolstering, as well as the subtle exceptions to that bright line rule that happens all the time in your interactions with a child who has alleged sexual abuse.

In today's case, the Defendant pointed to at least four witnesses who were allowed at trial to give testimony repeating the victim's disclosures regarding the molestation, which the Defendant argued reflected upon the consistency and credibility of the victim's statements.

(It should be noted that the victim in the case was 14 years old when she made disclosures, which means that under Georgia law the Child Hearsay Statute did not apply.

Here is the bright line bolstering rule, as set forth by the Georgia Court of Appeals in this case: "It is true that a witness's credibility may not be bolstered by the opinion of another, even an expert, as to whether the witness is telling the truth."

That is because credibility is a matter solely to be decided by the jury. A very limited exception relates to expert witnesses, who because of their expertise that is not held by the common layperson may be able to opine as to this ultimate issue of whether the witness is telling the truth. But that is very much the exception to the rule, and it was not present in today's case.

Therefore, the Court of Appeals decided that the Court erred when it allowed this testimony. But it also decided that despite the error, the Defendant was not prejudiced because he had an opportunity to cross-examine the victim to test her credibility. Further, the jury watched the forensic interview of the child, which allowed them to also assess the child's credibility. Finally, the Defendant was acquitted of two of the three child molestation offenses, which indicated to the Court of Appeals that the jury was able to objectively consider the evidence and the various charges.

But there was more to this case on the topic of bolstering, and this time the Court of Appeals found that the trial court did not commit error by allowing the testimony into evidence.

Specifically, the Court of Appeals addressed the Defendant's claims that (1) the forensic interviewer should not have been able to testify that the victim's "demeanor during the interview was consistent with her molestation allegations." and (2) the family counselor's testimony that the victim "was consistent with her allegations and did not appear to be vindictive"

Taking the forensic interviewer's testimony first, the Court of Appeals wrote: "It is not improper bolstering . . . for a witness to express an opinion as to whether objective evidence in the case is consistent with the victim's story."

Since the forensic interviewer's testimony addressed only her _objective observations of the victim's behavior_, rather than _whether she found the victim's statements believable or credible_, the testimony was properly admitted and not objectionable.

I think it is critical for the qualified lawyer of your choice in your state to research the law to see whether there are similar rules. In trainings I conduct in Georgia and elsewhere, the question often arises as to whether a witness, such a forensic interviewer or a counselor or a physician, should answer a question regarding whether a child exhibited signs consistent with a child who has been sexually abused. This type of testimony falls squarely under the rule in today's case—it's an example of a witness who testifies about her own objective observations of the child.

Whether it should be used at trial depends on a variety of factors, and should be thoroughly discussed prior to trial with the attorney who has subpoenaed you to determine whether it will in fact be part of your trial testimony. Used in the proper manner and in the proper situation, it can be powerful evidence, as it was in today's case.

The next bolstering evidence analyzed by the Court of Appeals was the family counselor's testimony that the victim, according to the testimony of the counselor at trial, "was probably the most consistent teenager that [she] had ever worked with concerning sexual abuse" and "had been the most consistent with her story," and "she never felt like [the victim] was being vindictive."

The Georgia Court of Appeals called this testimony "a closer question" as to whether it was improper. I agree. It is directly bolstering, stated as fact, and lacked any qualification language to indicate it was based upon objective observations.

It **must** be pointed out, that with proper pretrial preparation, testimony such as the above can be transformed from objectionable testimony to admissible testimony.

In this case, the defense lawyer did not object to the counselor's testimony, instead questioning her on cross examination about whether she had any "outside evidence" to support or refute the victim's story (answer: no), and whether it was the counselor's job to determine whether the victim's allegations were supported (answer: no). Thus, the Court of Appeals decided that trial counsel adequately addressed the counselor's testimony, and it was not insufficient assistance of counsel that he did not object.

Be prepared for this bolstering testimony issue. And as is my custom, I recommend that this and other topics that routinely occur in the courtroom be discussed with the attorney who is bringing you as a witness **before trial** when it can be thoroughly discussed.

Chapter Eight

How To Be A SuperWitness

Legal Eagles—I had the pleasure of presenting training sessions at the 11th Annual Child Abuse and Neglect Conference in Atlanta, which was sponsored by Children's Healthcare of Atlanta and the Stephanie V. Blank Center for Safe and Healthy Children.

My sessions were titled: "How to be a SuperWitness: And How to Feel Better About the Unknown Unknowns of Trial."

This is one of my favorite topics to discuss, because of the importance attached to having prepared, confident witnesses in any trial. I also understand that any witness of any category regardless of how many times he or she has testified, has concerns about testifying. And my rallying cry is always that any concern, great or small, should be addressed with the attorney calling the witness for trial **prior** to the testimony.

I won't go into the entire talk here, but I would like to speak mainly to one part of the discussion. This is what I know about witnesses—witnesses have the wrong perspective prior to their time of the stand. It's time to change the perspective!

Talk to people who are subpoenaed to testify soon and ask them what they are concerned about:

I'm nervous testifying.

I don't know if I'm prepared.

I don't know what I'll be asked on cross-examination.

I don't know if I will be credible.

I don't know what research the defense lawyer is going to ask me about.

I don't know what to say when I'm asked whether I believe the child.

I don't know if the jurors will like me.

If any of these are concerns of yours, then they're important. *Any* witness concern is important. The time to deal with concerns is well before the day you're on the stand. If you don't hear from the lawyer who has subpoenaed you well in advance of trial, then you, as a SuperWitness, will call that lawyer. If you get the lawyer's voice mail, then leave this simple message: Hi, this is me, your witness that you have subpoenaed. I have concerns about my testimony coming up."

That's all. That will get you a return call.

Then talk through your concerns—all of them. Don't take, "You'll do fine, don't worry" as an answer. Don't take, "You're only going to be on the stand briefly, it will be OK" as an answer. If you're important enough to be subpoenaed as a witness, then it's important enough to have all of your concerns addressed.

Of course, don't get snippy about it. But it should be conveyed that you take this responsibility of testifying at the trial of a child molestation case extremely seriously. Cursory preparation of witnesses, or brief assurances, is not what it takes to discharge this duty—whether it is the duty of the witness or the duty of the trial lawyer presenting the witness.

That said, please go back to the bullet points of concerns, and look to see what they all have in common.

What is it?

All of these concerns are witness-centered. All of these concerns are about you, the witness. Not one of them has anything to do with concerns of the most important people in the courtroom.

And so I believe that many, many (if not most) witnesses have the wrong perspective. I believe it's important to change the perspective from witness-centered to service-centered.

What in the world does that mean?

As a professional in the field you have chosen, you serve others. You serve your community. You help others. You help your community.

Therefore, one important step toward moving from a witness-centered perspective to a service-centered perspective is: Know who you are! First, I'll tell a story about knowing who you are! After, I'll tell you why it's important in the realm of witness testimony.

I tell the story in these "How to be a SuperWitness" trainings about the Crimes Against Children detective who my son and I ran into at a Barnes and Noble. We chatted inside the bookstore for a while, and then went our separate ways.

When my son and I left the store and went to our car, I looked in befuddlement at a flat tire on my car. Crap.

On the one hand, this could be a great father-son bonding experience. On the other hand, I change tires once in a blue moon. But onward I charged, hoping to instill good mechanical instincts into my middle-school-aged son.

Just then my favorite CAC detective walks by and says, "So you have a flat?" "Yeah," I said, "I got it though, don't worry." My favorite detective said, "I'm sure you do, but I'll hang around just in case."

Thank goodness. And of course, he ended up doing most of the work.

Because that's what he does. And that's what you do. You help. It's in your DNA, just like it was in the detective's DNA.

Know who you are! It is so important because you know exactly what one of the things that a cross-examining lawyer will try to do: Present you as someone you're not. Sloppy. Disorganized. Unprofessional. Uninformed. Whatever.

35

Be ready for it, and rely upon knowing who you are and how you help others in the community. Your DNA does not change just because you have walked into a courtroom.

And remember this: When you are brought into a case, which is well before you are subpoenaed as a trial witness, you are brought in not just to serve, but to be the calm one in the storm of activity that has occurred. You are brought in to, it is hoped, stabilize the situation. You are brought in to help in times of crisis.

Now fast-track to the courtroom. Who is it in the courtroom that needs help? Who are the people in the courtroom who are thrust into unfamiliar, uncomfortable, and emotional surroundings? Who is it in the courtroom that ultimately has the most important responsibility?

Right. The jurors. It is hoped that the SuperWitness will be able to help them reach an informed decision. And it is just as important for you to understand that while they need your help, they have their own very real concerns. Their concerns matter, too, a lot. That is why it is important to change from an inward witness-centered perspective to an outward service-centered perspective.

Your concerns are to be resolved prior to trial. Once that is done, the service-centered perspective is easier to achieve.

One last comment. When you help people, people feel safe. When the detective changed my tire, I knew that it was safe to drive away from the bookstore.

In jury trials, one of the important things that jurors consider throughout the course of the trial is what sounds safe to them. In the end, it seems, jurors are making decisions that depend on safety. If, throughout your day-to-day roles in this area of child sexual or physical abuse, you make safe decisions, it will translate into credible evidence at trial.

Day-to-day safe decisions run the gamut: from keeping tremendously professional records; to following standards and protocols; to relying on your skill, education and training; to relying on your good instincts; to being able to see the other side of the coin even when it is not supported by the evidence; and on and on.

The witness perspective can be changed. Try it, you might like it!

Chapter Nine

For Witnesses, It's the Fear of the Unknown

Legal Eagles—It's the fear of the unknown that is tough on so many witnesses. If you compound with a prior bad experience on the witness stand, or two, or three, then you have a recipe for the proverbial deer in the headlights.

But this topic really should involve the topic of a lawyer preparing witnesses for trial, and it goes straight to the heart of why so many people are intimidated by the thought of sitting on a witness stand and testifying in court. The fear of the unknown caused by inadequate trial preparation.

First, let's briefly talk about two cases to define the problem, and then I'll provide some suggestions for being prepared to testify in court.

Case #1: Bryant v. State, Georgia Court of Appeals, Case No. A10A0789, (Decided August 3, 2010).

Facts: The Defendant was indicted for aggravated sexual battery, aggravated sodomy, aggravated child molestation and child molestation related to alleged acts involving his 9-year-old stepsister. The acts allegedly occurred between December 31, 2004 and June 2, 2005.

The victim's mother was on the stand, testifying on cross-examination. The defense lawyer asked her whether she knew when the alleged molestation occurred. Her response raised the possibility that some of the alleged acts occurred after June 2, 2005, unbeknownst to anyone else in the courtroom. Part of her response was, "Yesterday there was a lot of stuff (that) came out at the psychologist that I did not know. She told the psychologist that it happened multiple times during the day, so I believe her."

You Legal Eagles can spot the problems with this testimony.

1. Hearsay: "She told the psychologist that it happened multiple times during the day." Hearsay (and really double hearsay)—it's what someone told someone else, and the "someone else" is not in the courtroom to testify about the child's comments first-hand.

But you might ask: What about the Child Hearsay Statute? Isn't that an exception? No, not in this case. The child's statement was not made directly to the mother, who could have then relayed the child's statement if it involved child sexual abuse (at least according to Georgia's Child Hearsay statute—your state may differ). Instead, the child's statement was apparently made to a third person (the psychologist) who was not the person who testified about the statement at trial. That causes the statement to be inadmissible, even under the Child Hearsay Statute.

2. Bolstering testimony. The mother concluded, "I believe her." No can do. The jury determines the credibility and believability of witnesses, including the alleged victim in this case.

But there is a more subtle problem with this testimony which can cause concerns, and in fact did cause concerns in this case. "Yesterday there was a lot of stuff (that) came out at the psychologist . . ."

"Yesterday." Uh-oh. If you're thinking like a lawyer, you're going through things in your head: *Trial is today. Yesterday, there was important information that involves the allegations of molestation. Did I know that? Did the opposing lawyer know that? Was the opposing lawyer entitled to know that through the discovery rules? Did I discuss this with my witness before putting her on the stand? Did I instruct my witnesses to keep me updated with all current circumstances that go to the heart of this case? Did I, on my own, contact my witnesses to see whether there are any updated circumstances that go to the heart of the case?*

Result: Mistrial. The defense counsel asserted that he had no notice that there was alleged molestation that occurred after June 2, 2005. According to the Court of Appeals opinion, "The trial court expressed dismay that the prosecution, defense counsel, and the court were learning about the child's recent trip to the psychologist on the first day of trial. The judge then asked defense counsel whether he wanted a mistrial. Defense counsel indicated that he did, and the trial court granted the request."

<u>Case # 2:</u> Goss v. State, Georgia Court of Appeals, Case No. A10A1578, (Decided August 3, 2010).

Facts: The Defendant was convicted of child molestation and aggravated sexual battery. He complained on appeal that his trial counsel provided ineffective assistance for failing to do a number of things, including failing to obtain certain documents.

As it relates to the documents, the Defendant complained on appeal that his lawyer failed to obtain DFACS (CPS) records, school records, medical records, mental health records, and the personnel records of the police officers involved, among other things.

Result: Conviction affirmed. The Court of Appeals denied Defendants appeal as it relates to the document issue because the Defendant's appeal failed to provide any argument or legal authority to support his document issue argument. But the case illustrates loud and clear that there are often signs that defense counsel will fail to adequately prepare for trial by, in this case, allegedly failing to obtain what might be important documents for use at trial.

In sum, we have seen evidence of incomplete preparation on both sides of the aisle in these two cases today.

So what can you do about it in order to be more comfortable and confident that you're prepared to testify?

The answer requires multiple discussions, which we have had in one form or another in past chapters. For purposes of this chapter, I will focus on just one important aspect—what you can do instead of waiting by the phone to be prepped by the lawyer who is calling you as a witness.

ONE: Let the lawyer who is calling you as a witness know that you do not believe you are fully prepared to testify, if in fact you believe that you are not fully prepared to testify. This tends to draw lawyers attention. If you feel this why, then don't be satisfied with a response such as, "You'll be fine. You've done this before." Each time is different, and each case is critical. Even the most seasoned witnesses have concerns. If you don't believe me, ask a veteran CAC detective.

TWO: Know why you are not fully prepared to testify, and be able to express it to the lawyer. Do you know the reason you are being called to testify? Do you know what facts you are being called on to show? Do you know what the issues are that the defense has focused on as it relates to your interaction with the child in the case? Do you know whether the defense has identified an expert to critique your work product? Is there anything in your file that worries you, in any way? Do you believe that the lawyer calling you as a witness fully understands the complete extent and scope of your involvement in the case?

THREE: I am putting this at three, but it should really be in place before **ONE**. The best-case scenario is to have a system where getting prepared for trial occurs well in advance of trial, in place. I am in civil trial practice, so I fully understand that my definition of "well in advance of trial" differs from a prosecutor's definition. It's just the nature of the two systems of justice, and the enormous caseloads many prosecutor's offices have. I have heard of and seen the situation where prosecutors who believe they are trying Case A on Monday, and when they show up on Monday—for one reason or another—they are told by the judge to be ready to try Case B. Incredibly hard.

But we also know that these situations are inevitable, so there are two ways we can address them. The first way is to believe that due to the nature of the criminal justice jury trial system, we just have to acknowledge that being fully prepared for trial might not occur in every case. The second way, which is the SuperWitness way, is to say "hogwash" because there is much that SuperWitnesses can do on their own to be prepared. A system can be put into place that case-tracks your files, and can tell you at what point, from indictment to trial, a case is in. For example, once a case reaches the point where it is first placed on a trial calendar, plans can be made to begin the trial preparation process. A system can be put into place to communicate with the prosecutor's office to determine the case status, and whether, in their best information, the case involving you is heading toward trial. That is the point to communicate any concerns you have, well ahead of the actual trial date.

FOUR: By discussing that "every witness has concerns," I am absolutely not stating that you should doubt your abilities. Everyone who has an interest in reading this book has one of the greatest advantages that there is for a witness, because everyone, in some shape or form, is in the business of assisting in safety. Safety is a concept that every person who serves as a juror wants, for themselves certainly, and hopefully for their family and community. When you have done your job in a way that places safety at the top, then it can lead to remarkably important testimony. There is much more to this topic, but I will leave it for another chapter or another edition. For purposes of this one, the important thing to stress is that when a witness realizes that she has testifying concerns, that recognition is a strength because it can be addressed before she raises her right hand and promises to tell the truth.

Chapter Ten

Multiple Relevant Purposes of Documents

Legal Eagles—One of the more maddening things for many witnesses is when lawyers explain to them that certain things that happen every day outside in the "real world" can't be used inside the courtroom because they are inadmissible due to some rule of evidence.

This is particularly grating when many of those things that happen outside in the real world are used by people to make good decisions every day. Take hearsay, as an example. A police officer, with 25 years of experience and 25 medals of commendation, witnesses an incident. He tells a fellow officer all about the incident, in spectacular detail. But if the first officer, for whatever reason, is unavailable for trial, and the second officer wants to convince a jury about the truth of the first officer's out-of-court statements, he can't. That's hearsay, and is generally admissible.

Ah, but I said "generally." That's the key. Rules of evidence can certainly take away, but they can also give back. An astute lawyer might look at the first officer's statement to the second officer, and despite the first officer being unavailable, find other evidentiary rules that would allow some—or even all—of the first officer's statements into evidence.

So as a SuperWitness, when a lawyer tells you that you can't introduce a statement, or a report, or something else that is tangible into evidence because "the rules of evidence don't allow it," I'd like you to say, "Can we use the statement (or document) (or something else that is tangible) for another purpose?"

You'll be off the charts!

Case: Black v. State, Georgia Court of Appeals, Case No. A10A1201, (Decided September 10, 2010).

Facts: The Defendant was convicted of child molestation and aggravated child molestation of his 11-year-old granddaughter. He was also accused of taking pictures of her with his camera. When his granddaughter told her parents what happened, the Defendant admitted taking naked pictures of his granddaughter, that he destroyed them, and that he wanted to kill himself.

At trial, an investigator with the County's Department of Family and Children's Services (DFACS) testified that she became involved after her office received an anonymous fax approximately six months after the incidents alleged occurred. The fax detailed allegations of the sexual abuse against the granddaughter, as well as sexual abuse of the Defendant's stepdaughter from another marriage.

The Defendant's sister-in-law sent the fax. At trial, the Defendant testified that he did not molest his granddaughter. Following his conviction, the Defendant appealed on numerous grounds, including his argument on appeal that the trial court erred by allowing the introduction into evidence of the anonymous fax.

Result: Conviction affirmed.

Good rule to know: The relevance of a piece of evidence can increase exponentially with a pre-trial analysis of how many different things can be proven with it. In other words, if the lawyer can't succeed under established rules of evidence at first, she should try again and again.

I think this particular case before us today was an easy call for the Court of Appeals, because the sister-in-law was available to testify and could authenticate the document. But let's assume the fax's author remained unknown through the time of trial. Total hearsay, and a shutout, right?

Initially, let's look at the Defendant's complaints related to the fax. First, the Defendant focused on the language of the fax that allegedly referred to victims other than the granddaughter. He argued that such information would inflame the jury, and prejudice his defense. He further argued on appeal that the trial court had even made a pre-trial ruling that would exclude such information.

However, here is where sloppy defense lawyering comes into play in cases. First, the Court of Appeals rejected the Defendant's argument on appeal because the faxed copy that was introduced into evidence redacted all information related to "other children." There was no such information in front of the jury!

Secondly, however, even if "other children" wasn't redacted from the fax that went out with the jury, the Defendant still would have lost this part of his appeal, again, due to sloppy lawyering. While the Defendant was correct that the trial court ruled that there could not be evidence of the abuse of other victims, the trial judge limited the "other victims" reference specifically to the Defendant's two daughters. The trial court made no ruling whatsoever related to any other people (other than his two daughters) that he might have victimized, apparently because the defense lawyer didn't ask for such a ruling.

That left the Defendant's other argument on appeal that the fax should not have been introduced into evidence—the catch-all "not relevant" argument.

Remember what relevance is as it relates to evidence.

As the Court of Appeals wrote: "Any evidence is relevant which logically tends to prove or disprove any material fact which is at issue in the case, and every act or circumstance serving to elucidate or throw light on a material issue is relevant."

Georgia (and likely your state) favors the admission of any relevant evidence, regardless of how slight its probative value may be. (Refresher: Probative = something that tends to prove a particular proposition.) Why? Because it allows the jury to fully weigh all of the evidence in making its decision.

The judge determines whether evidence is probative when she decides to allow it to be admitted in a case. After that, the jury goes to work.

In this case, the fax was used for something other than the actual statements contained in it. As we said earlier in this chapter, "it was used for another purpose."

What was it? At trial, the evidence was that the molestation occurred sometime in December, but DFACS and law enforcement did not become involved until the next July. Further, the mother of the victim testified that she did not call the police after her daughter's outcry.

Thus, the fax was relevant, in the words of the Court of Appeals, "to explain how law enforcement and DFACS became involved in the matter and to corroborate (the Defendant's) sister-in-law's testimony that she notified DFACS because she was afraid for other children."

Documents you prepare every day have a primary purpose—like proper documentation. But what about some other areas of relevance? When a document is placed in the file, for example, that makes a referral of a child alleged to have been sexually abused to a counselor for treatment that is also relevant, perhaps, to show that the child "exhibited signs consistent with a child who has been sexually abused." We know that this evidence, if true, is a great bit of evidence to introduce to jurors.

So be aware of other purposes that troll beneath the main reason for a document. It might just be the best exhibit the trial lawyer could have—an exhibit that has multiple relevant purposes.

Chapter Eleven

Talking About Witness Testimony, and Revisiting the SuperWitness

Facts: I have often urged Children's Advocacy Centers to obtain reliable legal counsel to assist in the legal issues that routinely arise and directly affect the operation of the CACs.

My belief is that obtaining a competent legal counsel is no longer a luxury that CACs cannot afford. You are in a profession where it is inevitable that critical decisions are going to be made inside of the courtroom. You are also in a profession where there is an increasing awareness and understanding by lawyers, including criminal defense lawyers and their experts, of CACs. This increased awareness has led lawyers to refine their strategies and tactics, based upon their experiences, based upon the law, and based upon their consultations with their experts. The result is a more effective approach to facing CAC's generally and CAC witnesses in particular.

It is time for CACs to be armed with reliable legal support! This support can also include advice about the proper and effective ways to testify in court. So with that: Return of the *SuperWitness*!

In one of the previous chapters "How to be a SuperWitness" is actually a revised chapter I wrote years ago, and have often presented it during conferences as a talk by the same title.

Here, I am going to revisit the topic, but in an abbreviated fashion by focusing on only three "tips" regarding testifying.

Tip #1: Think Outward, Not Inward. Talk to many soon-to-be witnesses about their concerns, and you will find that most concerns are "inward." Witnesses tend to worry about how they feel; how they are going to perform; how they are going to be treated by the lawyers; whether they have enough credentials and/or credibility to be believable to the jurors; whether they are going to be embarrassed on the stand; whether they are going to be properly prepared.

This is not to say these are not valid concerns. They are, and an attorney who properly and adequately preps his witness can adequately deal them with.

The Legal Eagles Guide for Children's Advocacy Centers, Part III

But if up to the time you reach the witness stand you are thinking "inward," then you are thinking incorrectly. This is not about you.

To stop thinking inward, start "preparing" for trial the day you open that file. Everything you, if you do it the correct way, will create confidence leading up to the inevitable day that you will be called to trial as a witness in *some* case. You don't know which case, but you know by doing it the correct way in *all* cases then you will be ready for *some* case.

What is the "correct" way, you ask? We'll get to that. But first, more on changing your perspective from "inward" to something else that is much more productive.

That leads to **Tip #2.** Change the perspective. Instead of staying in the "inward" maze, change the perspective to the witness who is like the parachuter, floating over the landscape, looking down and seeing *other* people's perspectives. And the main thing that perspective witnesses need to be concerned about is the perspective of the **jurors**.

Jurors are the deciders. I call them the "target audience." They decide what facts to believe, what witnesses to believe, and what not to believe. A witness's role, upon proper preparation by the lawyer, is to show them the facts.

I have always thought (well, maybe not *always*, but as I've gotten older) that one of the first steps toward showing facts to the jurors is to *understand* what they must be going through, sitting on a jury panel, deciding a child molestation case.

For you therapists on the Legal List—what do you think is going through their minds? How do you think they felt when they first learned that the case they were going to decide was not that run-of-the-mill car crash case, but a child molestation case. What a horrible feeling in the pit of their stomach that many of them must have felt.

So you see, the CAC witness must recognize the fears and concerns of the *jurors*, and must show them that the CAC witness is the calm one, the professional one that people in crisis turn to in times of extreme difficulty—just as when a non-offending caregiver arrives at a CAC with a small child who has alleged sexual abuse.

And we haven't even talked about what the *Defendant* must be thinking. Or the *defense lawyer* trying to keep his client out of prison, or even the *judge*, who has to make sure she doesn't commit legal error in the trial that would lead to an appeal.

In sum, everyone who has an active role in the trial process has *issues*. And CAC people are trained in calm. We are the calm ones!

Tip #1 and **Tip #2** lead to **Tip #3.** We want to try to avoid thinking inward (Tip #1) and we want to change our perspective (Tip #2), and in many ways we change our perspective by thinking about what *jurors* are going through. In many ways we change our perspective by trying to show jurors what valid facts are, and what credible sources of information are.

And that leads to **Tip #3**—think about how jurors make decisions.

What? How in the world do we know how jurors make decisions? We're not in the deliberation room at the close of evidence watching them!

True enough. But how do *you* make decisions? What are the things you consider before booking a hotel in an unfamiliar city? What are the things you consider before allowing your pre-teen or teenager spend the night at the home of a friend whose parents you have not yet met? Do you lock your house doors at night? If so, why?

We are conditioned to make the safe decision. We are conditioned to make the safe choice. Sometimes the safe decision seems innocuous—we buckle our seat belts without even thinking about it. (It only registers as safe when we hear about a seat belt that saved someone's life.) Other times we make safe decisions upon far more careful reflection.

But we are conditioned to make safe decisions, and safe decisions ensure our continued survival.

Many trial lawyers, not just me, believe that jurors weigh evidence and come down on the side of safety.

And if there is one thing that describes your professional role, it is safety. That should give you such confidence when you are called as a witness. Safety is what you do.

But guess what? It is a double-edged sword. That which given can be taken away. I tell my "safety-type" witnesses, "Don't blow it!" Don't blow it by doing the "unsafe" in your role as forensic interviewer, or therapist, or child and family advocate, or child protective service worker. From the day your file is opened to the day you walk into the courtroom, strive to do the "safe" thing in everything you do.

It is "safe" to have military precise files; it is "safe" to go to continuing education courses; it is "safe" to know the research of your field; it is "safe" to know and follow your standards and protocols; it is "safe" to know the legal rules and statutes that directly affect your role; it is "safe" to understand the court opinions that speak to what you do.

Three tips—I hope they help!

Chapter Twelve

A Top 5 List to Keep the CAC Machine Running Smoothly

Legal Eagles—We're going to take a chapter off from reviewing appellate cases and discuss a Top 5 list, which is designed to have a CAC run like a well-oiled machine.

Number 1: Who is the records gatekeeper? You know my theory of releasing records by now. It's "No, no, no (generally) unless a court says so." There are exceptions, as my "generally" qualification indicates, but that's for another chapter.

To understand the "why" of this rule, you have to understand the "what."

What records do we have on site at a CAC? First, records that are confidential by law because they involve allegations of child sexual abuse and/or child physical abuse. In Georgia, those records are confidential by statute (i.e., a law passed by the state legislature), and can be found in O.C.G.A. § 49-5-40 et seq. In your state outside of Georgia, you almost certainly have such a statute, which can be easily researched by the attorney of your choice. There are also federal statutes that trigger such confidentiality.

What else do we have at our CAC? Counseling records, which usually trigger issues of client privilege. I say "usually" because your state's privilege statute is going to list the types of professionals who can maintain the counseling privilege with the client. For example, in Georgia the professionals include Ph.D., LCSW, LPC, M.D., and some others.

What other records do we have at our CAC? We can obtain records that originated outside of our four walls. For example, some centers, through the MDT approach, may end up with law enforcement-type records, or medical records, or even school records. A non-offending caregiver may bring records to the Center that are then placed in the file. The importance of this? It means that if a request for "any and all documents in any form related to (the subject child)" comes into the CAC, such a request means "any and all documents in any form," including the records that did not originate with the CAC. Thus, those other entities, such as law enforcement, or the medical facility, etc., probably

47

did not get notice that their records were being sought. If provided with proper notice, they might want to file their own objection on behalf of their department or facility.

So who is the gatekeeper, the person who will funnel every request for records that comes through the doors, without fail? The gatekeeper helps keep the CAC from releasing records that should not be released unless a judge says so.

But we know that requests come in other forms. So that leads to Number 2.

Number 2: Who is the keeper of the telephone "request" line? Requests often come via the old telephone, many times by lawyers, or their clients, or people who have no lawyer. Many of these requesters genuinely believe that they are entitled to records, and don't understand that there are procedural requirements for obtaining many of them (as described above in **Number 1.**)

If there is one rule you should know about lawyers, it's that they want your stuff. Some lawyers, even those who know that there might be certain procedural requirements that must be ticked off the list before obtaining the records, still might not care to worry about them. And sometimes there is a misunderstanding that just because a child of their client was seen at a CAC, the non-offending caregiver can obtain any records related to their children.

A telephone response has to be consistent and clear. The best situation is where the record gatekeeper is also the telephone "request" line responder. What the response entails should be discussed with the CAC lawyer, but in short it should be, well, short. For example, there is a procedure for obtaining records, and any requests for records should be submitted in written form, which will then be forwarded to the CAC lawyer for review. Again, the right response for your CAC can be established with the assistance of legal counsel.

For requests that solely relate to counseling records that originated with the CAC by the CAC therapist, there can be a discussion with the CAC lawyer to ensure the most efficient manner of producing the records, which of course will still apply with all applicable laws.

Number 3: Who is your Center's go-to lawyer? I don't have to tell you that CACs are professionally run organizations, staffed with people who have unique skill sets that have been obtained through years of experience, years of higher education, or both. Many times at trial, an enormous amount of reliance is placed on those who work in CACs, and often their encounters with children, in one form or another, are critical to the court proceedings. Further, many times, on the strength of this testimony, life-changing decisions are made by jurors.

I have seen first-hand through reviewing appellate cases involving child molestation that the court system generally views CACs as expert organizations. True, there have been lows with regard to poor CAC testimony reviewed in some appellate decisions, but the vast majority of the cases I have read involve cases where ultimately the appellate court has endorsed the professionalism of those who have testified from a CAC.

The Legal Eagles Guide for Children's Advocacy Centers, Part III

Where am I going with this? If CACs are seen as professional organizations, then the legal system is going to expect that the entirety of a CAC's response to legal matters are done in a professional manner. CPS has attorneys responding for them in Court. Medical organizations have attorneys responding for them in Court. Many doctors, therapists and counselors in private practice have attorneys responding for them in Court. Legal representation, despite the bad PR lawyers may receive in the stereotypical sense, allows the justice system to move matters more efficiently. And the person in charge of the courtroom—the judge—appreciates this.

And so I say it again: obtaining competent legal counsel to handle these issues should not be seen as "a luxury that we cannot afford," or "a piece of the puzzle that we just don't need."

Once a competent and qualified lawyer is hired, you will feel the weight of the world release from your shoulders. No longer does your director, or your therapist, or your forensic interviewer, or your child and family advocate have to navigate what can be seen as perilous waters. Instead, these matters are sent to the lawyer for response.

I have the privilege of working for some CACs, and I have a confession to make even though it pains me to admit.

It isn't hard work. In fact, for a lawyer with a civil trial practice, it is positively easy work, once you understand the handful of statutes that are involved, and the typical lawyer tactics that CACs encounter. You should know this when hiring a lawyer—he is not analyzing international transactions involving Chinese monetary policy—so he shouldn't be paid like it! And a further discounted fee for working for an organization that assists alleged child sexual abuse victims is in order. Make sure she understands that. Pretty soon, your lawyer will be working for free, happily or otherwise.

Number 4: What is the system for notifying your CAC's lawyer of every legal request for records that the gatekeeper has obtained? Requests for records have time deadlines, as we all know. Subpoenas, requests for production for documents, lawyer letters demanding records, court orders—they all make the same sound: *tick, tick, tick.*

We want to diffuse them properly before they go boom!

A request in any form for records continues to tick until it is properly responded to, meaning in a legal way. There is a name for the letter response sent by the CAC director back to the lawyer who has subpoenaed CAC records. It is called a "letter." It is not a legal response.

Your lawyer's CAC needs to be notified promptly of all demands for records—I like e-mails, faxes and phone calls (office and mobile)—so that the proper and timely response can be made.

Number 5: What kinds of meetings and discussions occurred regarding the legal issues affecting your center? Practicing law is in at least one respect like practicing medicine. Preventative medicine is a nice goal for your health, and preventing legal time bombs from exploding is nice for your CAC.

Your lawyer will not mind putting on the bomb detonation clothes if he has to, but the better practice is for a CAC to forward their lawyer some legal subjects to discuss periodically, and even request their lawyer to conduct periodic in-service trainings. Or CACs in a geographical area can combine forces and bring in a lawyer who might be working at one of the nearby centers. When these in-service trainings happen, there is never a problem with taking questions from the floor; there are always questions to address.

Chapter Thirteen

The CAC's "Eight Iron"

<u>Case:</u> Pareja v. State, Georgia Court of Appeals, Case No.: 295 Ga. App. 871, (Decided February 10, 2010).

<u>Facts</u>: We have written about this very important Georgia case before.

It involved a defendant accused of molesting the 5-year-old daughter of his and his wife's friend.

At trial, a psychologist in private practice testified about the disclosures the girl made during the course of counseling. The psychologist, a mandated reporter, reported her suspicions of child sexual abuse to child protective services, called the Department of Family and Children Services in Georgia. The CPS case manager actually interviewed the Defendant, who told her that he wiped the child "to clean her" after she complained that she was "itchy."

But it is the CAC's involvement in the case, and the Court of Appeal's discussion of its records, that is critically important for CACs in Georgia, and very likely in your state.

As we start a new year, it is worth revisiting and remembering an important tool.

I know everyone on this list has all kinds of time to play golf. I'm not a golfer, but I want to offer an anecdote about a former world-class golfer named Curtis Strange.

Curtis Strange I believe was No. 1 in the world at one time. He wasn't the best driver, he didn't hit the best irons, and he wasn't the best putter. But he was ridiculously consistent, and so he was always near the top of the finishers of most tournaments.

So a reporter interviewed him about his success, and the very fact that he wasn't the most talented in any one discipline needed for golfers to be successful.

His answer was his 8 iron.

His 8 iron, for him, was automatic. He could do anything he wanted to the golf ball with an 8 iron, and he could put the golf ball wherever he wanted to put it. His 8 iron was his "go-to" club for success. In fact, he would hit other shots so that they fell within his 8 iron range. Once in 8 iron range, he was home free.

The rule in Pareja v. State is a Georgia CAC's 8 iron. For you Legal Eagles in other states, the attorney of your choice will be able to research, and it is hoped, find the Pareja v. State equivalent in your state.

So while we've talked about Pareja before, I think it is best if we are went back to basics.

To understand the importance of Pareja, it is important to acknowledge that the main way your CAC will be initiated into a litigation as a third party, whether civil or criminal, is through requests and demands for the information housed at your Center. (Remember, a "third party" means someone or some entity who is not one of the Plaintiffs or Defendants in civil cases, or who is not a Defendant in a criminal case.)

Receiving a subpoena for documents in a criminal case has the tendency to worry the recipient of it, or at least cause some unease.

Get out your 8 iron!

In Pareja, the Defendant appealed his conviction, in part on the fact that his defense attorney failed to subpoena the child's case file from the CAC. The argument on appeal was that this was ineffective assistance of counsel, because his lawyer could have obtained information from it that could have assisted in the defense.

The Georgia Court of Appeals weighed in, and in doing so, set the ground rules for subpoenas that are served upon Georgia CACs in any litigation, whether civil or criminal.

The 8 iron was taken out of the golf bag right away, as the Court wrote:

> "First, we note that the (Children's Advocacy) Center's file was confidential and not subject to direct subpoena by Pareja."

Boom. That case, from 2010, changed the way I have responded for the CACs I do work for every single time. Generally speaking, I won't even file a Motion to Quash the subpoena. Instead, I send a simple letter to the subpoenaing attorney, and explain to him or her (politely and professionally) that the subpoena is insufficient to obtain the CAC records directly from the CAC. A subpoena served directly from a lawyer to a CAC for a CAC's confidential records is simply not the right tool in the lawyer's tool bag to get the records.

Then I cite the language from the Court of Appeals in Pareja:

> "The proper procedure for obtaining access to such records in cases such as the one at bar is to petition the trial court to subpoena the records and conduct an in camera inspection as to whether the records are necessary for determination of an issue before the court and are otherwise admissible under the rules of evidence"

Formula: Lawyer who wants CAC confidential records requests the Court to issue an order or a subpoena to the CAC that instructs the CAC to send the confidential records directly to the Court for the Court's inspection.

In almost two years of doing this since the Pareja case was issued, I have never received any push back from an attorney. In fact, to a "T," the attorneys have not heard about Pareja, have not considered the confidential nature of CAC records, and seek some kind of guidance as to how to proceed forward to properly and legally obtain the records.

It is my 8 iron. Comfortable. Dependable.

But you know, even Curtis Strange must have hit a bad 8 iron shot, at least once or twice, don't you think?

Legal Eagle Rule No. 1. Don't get complacent. Know the rules of the road, which will be known once you obtain competent and qualified legal counsel of your choice.

Before I hit this Pareja 8 iron, I need to make sure that; in fact, the attorney is subpoenaing confidential information. If the information being subpoenaed is not confidential, then my letter has all the value of 2-cent stamp.

What makes the records confidential in Georgia is that they relate to allegations of child sexual or physical abuse. That triggers the confidentiality rules of a particular Georgia statute (a/k/a law) that specifically states that such records are confidential. If that statute is not triggered by a subpoena request, than I can't object to the release of records on that ground.

In summary, I suggest that you and your CAC (or you and your organization if outside the CAC realm) take an inventory of the areas in which you and your organization are brought into the legal world. There are only so many creatures out there that will draw you in, and all of them (subpoenas, requests for production documents, authorizations, etc.) have rules and response mechanisms.

There should be no mystery as to how to respond, so I urge your CAC to obtain a counsel and her 8 iron to help you.

Chapter Fourteen

Are We Up To Task of Our "Teachable Moment" Opportunity?

Legal Eagles—Scan your newspaper's opinion pages, your local blogs, or your media outlets in your communities.

Do you see opinion pieces and letters to the editors related to the facts, conditions and realities of child sexual abuse in your communities?

Do you see information supplied by child advocate organizations—either local, state or national—speaking to the important issues you face every day when supporting children who have alleged child sexual abuse or severe physical abuse?

We were in what many people refer to as a "Teachable Moment" phase, in light of Penn State and now Syracuse University. As details emerged—and as the lawyer for Jerry Sandusky inexplicably let his client speak publicly—child-service-centered organizations had an important opportunity and even a critical chance to properly inform the public of what you professionals face each and every day.

I want to encourage your organization to submit a column or a letter to the editor of your local newspaper. The points for your topics to discuss are all around us right now.

For example, I note the Penn State Statement of Trustees, in response to the Sandusky allegations. I have experience in bringing civil claims on behalf of children who were abused by employees or volunteers of child-service organizations, and have seen statements from these organizations released to the media. Usually, these statements express shock and concern, before discussing the long history of the organization's commitment to family and community. They then discuss how the organization will cooperate with authorities, how they properly screen their employees, and how they had no notice that the employee could cause harm, if he in fact caused harm at all. This is not a critique of these very difficult responses to tragic circumstances. But ultimately, I am struck by the lack of discussion about any harm caused to the children, or the impact of abuse against children in our communities.

But the Penn State statement was different. If you haven't read it, Google "Penn State Abuse Statement." I'll highlight the first paragraph.

The Legal Eagles Guide for Children's Advocacy Centers, Part III

> "The Board of Trustees of The Pennsylvania State University is outraged by the horrifying details contained in the Grand Jury Report. As parents, alumni and members of the Penn State Community, our hearts go out to all of those impacted by these terrible events, especially the tragedies involving children and their families. We cannot begin to express the combination of sorrow and anger that we feel about the allegations surrounding Jerry Sandusky. We hear those of you who feel betrayed and we want to assure all of you that the Board will take swift, decisive action."

For me, the language in the first paragraph is the language to highlight for its importance and candor. It is also refreshing to see a good organization acknowledge that even in their organization, bad things can happen to children, and it is the organization's responsibility to support the children in a consistent manner.

Finally, as the curtain comes down on our fourth year of the Legal Eagles, I want to express my respect and admiration for all you have chosen to do for children and their families in need.

Chapter Fifteen

The Records Request Dilemma—To Give or Not to Give?

Legal Eagles—To give records, or not to give? That is at the top of the list of questions I get from CAC folks.

I start with the general proposition, "No, unless a judge says so." I start from this proposition because of the various statutes that make records that tend to be in a CAC's possession confidential, privileged, or a combination of both.

But that leaves some circumstances unanswered. What happens if the request for records comes in the form of what appears to be a valid authorization, notarized for that extra sizzle? Or what if the request comes at a time where there is no court case pending? After all, if there is no court case, there can be no judge to say so, right?

Those circumstances will remain unanswered for now. For purposes of this Legal Letter, I'd like to discuss a very recent case that again supports the general "No, unless a judge says so" rule.

Importantly, today's case is a procedure-changer for Georgia CACs. Cases that affect an organization's procedures only come along every once in a while, so please take note.

As always, the rules discussed in Georgia cases may have application to your state as well. Your lawyer of choice will have to research a few statutes to make her determination for you, and to decide whether today's Georgia case will at a minimum be a good road map for other states.

Case: Waters v. State, Georgia Court of Appeals, Case No. A09A1980, (Decided March 26, 2010).

Facts: The Defendant was convicted of molesting his 3 ½ year old granddaughter. The victim complained to her mother that her grandfather gave her a "boo boo," pointing to her vagina. A pediatrician examined the child the next day, and while noticing redness determined that it was inconclusive as to evidence of molestation.

However, child protective services (DFACS in Georgia) became involved, and referred the child to a children's advocacy center for a forensic interview. Police interviewed the grandfather, telling him that he would be notified if a criminal warrant was issued. Two days later, the grandfather purchased a one-way ticket to Costa Rica. He was arrested two months later while re-entering the U.S., and was ultimately tried, convicted, and sentenced to 20 years in prison.

On appeal, the Defendant argued that the State's prosecutor did not properly comply with discovery, i.e., the pretrial procedure of exchanging documents, photographs, tangible objects, etc. with the defense attorney. Specifically, the Defendant argued that during trial, he discovered for the first time that the victim had a counselor who had conducted additional sessions of which he was not aware. The Defendant blamed the prosecutor for not turning those session notes over during the discovery process.

Result: Conviction affirmed.

Good rules to know: This case has two critical rules to know and understand, both for counselors who work for CACs and for private practice counselors.

First, I'll discuss prosecutorial duties related to criminal discovery in Georgia. Remember our Legal Eagle mission—Legal Eagles must have an advanced understanding of the legal rules that affect their day-to-day practice, including legal rules that might apply to professionals (such as prosecutors in this instance) outside of their fields, so long as those legal rules can indirectly or directly impact them.

During what is known as "reciprocal" discovery, prosecutors have to provide information to the defense that the prosecutors are going to use in their main case or in rebuttal of the defense case, so long as that information is in the prosecutor's "possession, custody or control."

Georgia law also makes clear that the prosecutor has to make an attempt to acquire the information that is required to be produced in discovery. That is, the prosecutor cannot say that since the information is not currently within her possession, she does not have an affirmative duty to attempt to acquire it if she can.

Thus, the question arises: Does that duty to attempt to acquire such information apply to counseling notes by a CAC counselor or a private practice counselor, when that counselor provides services related to the underlying allegations of child sexual abuse? Great question!

Before I answer it, there is some background to discuss, related to the interaction between CAC folks and law enforcement, and between CAC folks and the district attorney's office. In Georgia, I have been adamant in my position when representing CACs in court that the CACs are separate and distinct from law enforcement and the DA's office. It is a well-worn strategy for the defense to either imply or state explicitly that CAC professionals are mere rubber stamps for the prosecution. It is a bias attack that is such a routine that it should be no surprise.

CACs pros are not rubber stamps! They must be objective, independent and professional, and follow standards and protocols in order to carry out their responsibilities. They must understand that the DA's office is not staffed with CAC legal representatives. The DA's office is staffed with attorneys who work on behalf of the State of Georgia (or Kentucky)(or California)(or New Jersey).

Today's case makes that point directly. The State's position was that "[T]here was no duty for the State to affirmatively seek the therapist's work product, and that it had not seen any of the information contained in the counselor's therapy reports."

The Court of Appeals agreed. The court held that "[C]ontrary to the Defendant's contentions, the . . . discovery act does not provide an independent statutory basis for the discovery of the therapist's files."

In sum, Rule 1: Prosecutors have no duty under Georgia's reciprocal discovery law to affirmatively obtain the notes of counselors or therapists who treat the alleged sexual abuse victim. An important offshoot of this rule is that counselors and therapists of CACs, and private practice counselors and therapists, are not rubber stamps!

That leads to Rule 2 of the case, and the rule that I believe sets a new procedure for counselors who treat alleged sexual abuse victims, and whose records are subpoenaed as part of litigation.

Preliminarily, in my previous books, I've described at various times Georgia's law related to records and reports of child abuse. Many of you have this statute tattooed on your forehead: O.C.G.A. § 49-5-40 et seq., which by law in Georgia makes reports of alleged child sexual abuse confidential, and requires that access to those records are done only on a very, very limited basis. It also provides that CACs can obtain such records (which they do, e.g., from law enforcement or child protective services or M.D.'s), but that CACs cannot release these confidential records except under very limited circumstances.

I have written in the past that it is incumbent upon CAC professionals in other states to have the lawyer of their choice research their state laws to see whether there is a similar statute, which is likely.

Moreover, in February 2009, in Pareja v. State (673 S.E.2d 343), the Georgia Court of Appeals laid down a rule that an attorney (whether it is a criminal defense lawyer or a plaintiff's lawyer or defense lawyer in a civil case) could not serve a subpoena directly on a Georgia CAC's for the CAC's forensic file.

That is, the Court of Appeals held that under O.C.G.A. § 49-5-40 et seq., and particularly § 49-5-41(a)(2), the proper procedure is for an attorney to request that the trial court issue a subpoena to the CAC, compelling the CAC to produce the forensic file to the Court so that the court could conduct an *in-camera* (in her chambers) inspection of these confidential records.

The inspection would be the judge's opportunity to determine whether the records were relevant to the issues in the case, and whether they would be released to the parties.

The Legal Eagles Guide for Children's Advocacy Centers, Part III

I said in February 2009 that Pareja v. State was a game-changer. It stated that a subpoena demanding forensic files served directly on CAC by an attorney is invalid. At the time, I wondered whether the Pareja v. State rule applied to CAC counseling records. It wasn't specifically addressed in Pareja.

Houston, we have our answer.

In today's Waters v. State case, the counseling records for the child were analyzed by the Georgia Court of Appeals through the lens of O.C.G.A. § 49-5-40 et seq., which is the exact statute that applies to the confidential nature of records concerning reports of child abuse that was analyzed in Pareja v. State.

The Court of Appeals stated that, "Thus, as Waters did not request an in camera inspection of [the therapist's] records . . . the State was not obligated to produce the file and did not violate his due process rights under . . . Georgia's reciprocal discovery act by not providing the file earlier."

I'm going to read one other thing into today's case, due to some of the language in the Court's quote that I just cited. I do not believe, even if the Defendant requested that the trial court conduct an *in camera* inspection of the therapy records, that the prosecutor would have a duty to produce the therapy file. Instead, it would be the therapist's duty to provide the file to the Court for the *in camera* inspection.

After all, the therapy file does not just contain confidential records of child abuse under O.C.G.A. § 49-5-40, but privileged information based upon the counseling relationship between the therapist and her client. Thus, the therapist would be the one responding to the *in camera* order, not the prosecutor, which is important because the therapist could then bring issues of counseling privilege to the court's attention as part of the entire analysis the trial judge would have to undertake.

One last very important note: Your Center's lawyer of choice will be able to research your home state for statutes and case law that will determine the proper procedure for your Center. This is one of the most important legal procedures for your Center to know about. If you and others at your Center are unclear, take that first step to get legal assistance to find out.

Whew. There is some heavy lifting in this chapter, but nevertheless this case is very important. The importance of it is that it goes a long way toward protecting a child's therapy records from unhindered demands.

Chapter Sixteen

Can That Forensic Interview DVD be Released to the Public?

Legal Eagles—In the past I have had a number of emails sent to me regarding the legal "status" of DVDs of forensic interviews of children. Particularly, the queries center on whether the F.I. DVD is a "public record" that may be disseminated, including to the media as part of its media coverage of child abuse proceedings.

My answer has two parts. After I give you the first part, bear with me—I don't like it either. But after I give it, I'll give you the second part.

The first part is: Yes, a DVD of a forensic interview of a child can be ordered by a judge to be released to the media that is covering a child abuse proceeding.

This happens when those who have an opportunity to file unequivocal, well researched, and timely objections to the overbroad distribution of the F.I. DVD at the first notice that such a request may occur fail to do so.

This is the second part. One theme throughout any child molestation prosecution is the important interest of protecting the alleged victim. There are many people who share this interest, including those who work within the Children's Advocacy Center, to the law enforcement investigators, to the prosecutor's office, to the non-offending parents or caregivers of the children. And of course, the final person, who can guarantee reasonable protections, is the trial judge before whom the case is tried.

"Informed anticipation" is an extremely important trait for those who participate in the trial process to possess. Lawyers particularly need to be able to anticipate the legal issues that not only most certainly will arise, but also may likely arise.

And along those lines, it should be no surprise to any lawyer or any CAC professional that a forensic interview will be sought during the course of the trial or pre-trial process.

Thus, standard pre-trial motions can be filed, either by the prosecutor or by the CAC lawyer whose CAC has been subpoenaed for its forensic interview DVD. This is a common tactic we use in responding to requests or demands for forensic interviews, with the pertinent language in the motion to request that the F.I. DVD, whether used or not as part of the proceedings, be sealed from public view and not released for use to any outside individuals, parties or organizations.

There are state statutes, in any state, supporting the confidential nature of such information. Further, there is abundant case law, both at the state and federal levels, including from the U.S. Supreme Court, that stands for the law and policy considerations of (1) keeping certain materials sealed from public view and (2) protecting innocent children from privacy and other substantive violations.

There are many readily apparent reasons that lawyers and CACs should possess "informed anticipation" that the disclosure of F.I. DVDs will be requested: more publicity about child molestation cases; more aggressive defense lawyering; more media interest, including non-traditional media outlets that actively seek "shock" materials; cases that actually have resulted in the release of such materials; and others.

One more comment. Most of the time, records involving the alleged sexual abuse of a child, including investigative records, records related to medical and counseling treatment, and the F.I. DVD are disseminated to the parties without the input of the child's own personal legal representatives. If the argument is to be made that the dissemination of such materials to the media, including the F.I. DVD, can permanently harm a child—and that argument must be made—then the notice and opportunity to make such an argument should also be given to the legal counsel who directly represents the child's interests.

Chapter Seventeen

Receiving a Court Order and Reacting

Legal Eagles—A little known fact to lie on people, and some lawyers for that matter, is that many Court Orders are drafted by lawyers, who then present the proposed order to the assigned judge for his or her signature. If the judge approves of the draft, she signs it and it is filed by the Clerk of Court.

In many jurisdictions, this is a perfectly valid procedure, because it saves the Court from having to draft an order for each and every of the dozens or hundreds of matters that might come before the judge each year.

But it also can lead to Orders that do not properly take into account of all of the laws that are triggered by the legal issues. It can lead to Orders that are one-sided, in favor of the party whose attorney drafted it. And it can also lead to Orders where some individuals and entities that are impacted—like Children's Advocacy Centers, for example—do not have an opportunity to be heard before the judge who signs the Order.

Real life example: A judge signs an order, ordering the local CAC to copy a forensic interview DVD and provide it not to the Court, but directly to the lawyer for one of the child's parents who is involved in a pending domestic dispute. The lawyer who drafted the order served a copy of the signed order on the CAC, with the question: When can I pick up the forensic interview DVD?

Any ideas? Let's first go with the basics.

The first thing to do when your Center gets anything legal is to contact its lawyer that day, by phone, email, fax, text, and let him know you got something legal. Don't let it sit for one day. This is a same-day assignment. Once the legal document, whatever it is, is sent to the lawyer, the lawyer can see the nature of the document and any deadline that the document requires.

I have often said that a Court Order that requires CACs to provide documents or records in its possession is the gold standard. What I mean by that is that the CAC is protected from any complaints that it has released confidential records once it has been ordered to do so by a judge. Without a court order, the CAC can be on shaky ground for releasing records in its possession in many instances. We've discussed these instances many times before.

Thus, for me, the general rule of releasing records maintained by CACs is expressed thusly: "Generally, no, no, no, says so." Of course, there are exceptions to the general rule, which will not discussed for purposes of this chapter.

But in the case I've highlighted above, the CAC did receive a Court Order, ordering that the CAC release the records to the attorney. So we're good, right? That falls into the ". . . unless a Court says so" doesn't it?

Sorry for this answer. Yes and no. *(A quick aside: the following analysis involves Georgia law, but your state may have similar rules regarding the confidentiality of records related to alleged child sexual abuse. The competent and qualified lawyer of your CAC's choosing will be glad to research it for you.)*

In Georgia, forensic interview DVDs of children fall under a statute found at O.C.G.A. § 49-5-41 et seq., which has a specific and important section at §49-5-41(a)(2), which reads:

> ". . . [T]he following persons or agencies shall have reasonable access to such records concerning reports of child abuse: . . . (2) A court, by subpoena, upon its finding that access to such records may be necessary for determination of an issue before such court; provided, however, that the court shall examine such record in camera . . ." (Underlined portion added by me.)

So quick recap—we have an order drafted by a lawyer and signed by a judge that by the terms of the order makes the CAC produce the DVD of the forensic interview directly to the lawyer instead of the judge for an *in-camera* inspection.

My Flags:

1. It bypasses the above code section. The judge is supposed to be the gatekeeper of records related to allegations of child sexual abuse. She reviews the DVD first, and then decides whether it will be released. And importantly, if the judge finds that the DVD should be released to the parties, the judge can place restrictions on the further dissemination of the DVD. We don't want forensic interviews floating around among lawyers and other people who have nothing to do with the case.
2. What is being released to the attorney instead of the judge for an *in-camera* is not the CAC's work product. It is law enforcement's. Law enforcement probably didn't get notice of the Order either, and thus have no opportunity to object. Law enforcement may have reasons—like a pending criminal investigation—that would like to bring to the Court's attention. Let me be clear, however. A judge in an unrelated domestic case can, has, and many times will review a forensic interview as part of his domestic case and release it to the lawyers, despite what law enforcement argues.

3. It's an order drafted by a lawyer that is not just legally inadequate, it also sets a bad precedent in that jurisdiction. We don't want orders coming at us left and right that are not in compliance with the statute. We have to try to figure out how to inform the particular judge in this case that he signed an order that contradicts the proper procedure set out in a statute passed by the state's legislature.

My Solutions:

1. First, when there's one lawyer in the case, there's probably another. Maybe two more, if there's a guardian ad litem involved. Have they seen the order? The CAC lawyer can find out who the other lawyers are, contact them, and ask very professionally and matter-of-factly:

   - Have you seen the Order?

   - Do they know that the order requires the CAC to turn over materials that are confidential, and didn't follow the proper procedures?

   - Was there a hearing on this before the Order was signed? If so, do you know why we weren't notified? If not, do you know why not?

   Sometimes by notifying the other lawyers, they will (as was done in this particular case) get on the train and notify the Court of the problem with the Order, which will allow the judge to vacate the order and instead go through the proper procedure.

2. Since it's a forensic interview, which is law enforcement work product, and because law enforcement probably didn't hear about it, I get my CAC contact to notify the investigating officer to let him or her know about the Order. Remember, most Orders are not sealed. They are open records that can be discussed, so there is nothing wrong with notifying law enforcement about the Order. It will then be up to the investigator and her department to take any steps to address issues related to the police investigation.

3. If the case involves multiple proceedings, including a criminal proceeding that is in litigation, I get my CAC contact to notify the assigned ADA, for the same reasons set forth in No. 2, above.

4. And of course, the CAC's lawyer, if no one else will, can consider filing a Motion for Reconsideration, setting out the proper procedure as set forth in the statute. This allows the case at hand to be completed properly, and then (hopefully) the next time a similar order comes across the judge's desk, it might not get signed.

In sum, Orders most of the time *are* the gold standard. But there can be reasons to seek an additional Order to get things *back in order* in your jurisdiction.

Chapter Eighteen

Lawsuits Against CACs? Take action!

<u>Facts</u>: In this chapter we'll talk a little bit about the types of lawsuits that could be brought against CACs, and what can be done to assist your CAC's lawyer in defending the claim.

It is important to know that anyone can file a lawsuit. That does not mean it's a winner. The issue is whether it is legally defensible or not.

First, the lawyer hired to defend a CAC in litigation against it is going to be hired by the CAC's commercial liability carrier. This means that, as can happen, the lawyer hired by the commercial carrier may not be completely up to speed regarding CACs, or even have any familiarity at all.

As an example, just because I routinely do work for various CACs in Georgia does not mean that I will be the lawyer defending the Centers if a lawsuit is filed against any one of them. In fact, I would not be defense counsel in such a claim. That is because the defense of any lawsuit is contractually governed by the commercial liability policy that exists between the liability insurer and the CAC. The liability insurer is contractually required to hire legal counsel and defend the lawsuit.

What does this all mean? First, it is very likely that the affected CAC will need to educate the attorney who is hired to defend the CAC! Please understand that this does not mean that the insurance carrier is hiring an incompetent lawyer or law firm to defend the CAC. It just means that the lawyer will likely not immediately understand CACs.

Does this sound familiar? Of course it does! Many, many lawyers and judges across the U.S.A. still, to this day, are not entirely familiar with CACs. So it will not be out of the ordinary that the lawyer defending a CAC will have a bit of a learning curve.

So in a case against a forensic interviewer, for example, it is important that the CAC and forensic interviewer start by providing materials regarding interview protocols to the attorney. Rest assured, the attorney will sooner or later find it, but the key is to find it sooner, not later.

Additionally, a CAC should have at its fingertips the names and the specific contact individuals of state and national organizations that can serve as clearinghouses of information for the lawyer.

With all of that said, as a former journalist, I have done what is known as "buried the lead." Journalists are trained to put the crux of the matter at the top of the newspaper article, not "buried" somewhere in the middle.

So I buried the lead. The first thing to do when a lawsuit is filed and served is Don't Freak Out!

Remember, I'm a Plaintiff's lawyer. I file the lawsuits. I know a freaked-out Defendant when I see him. I know that when a Defendant concentrates on his freak-out, there is likelihood that he will make mistakes during the course of discovery, even despite the best efforts of legal counsel to contain him.

Know this: Just because a lawsuit is filed doesn't mean it has legal merit. And even if the lawsuit has legal merit, it does not mean that there are adequate facts for the lawsuit to prevail.

I have said this before in the book, however, that it is important not to minimize the lawsuit as a stereotyped "jackpot justice" lawsuit filed by a greedy Plaintiff's lawyer. If you want this to be a morality play, I will tell you that there are many Plaintiffs' lawyers who will gladly accommodate you. And in the right case, I'm one of them.

Instead, it's back to basics for CACs facing these lawsuits. Remember that as a matter of routine, We Are The Calm Ones! We are the ones who prepare small children and their non-offending caregivers for the great unknowns of what happens after an allegation of child abuse occurs. We help them see that there is hope, and light at the end of the tunnel. Once a lawsuit is filed against a CAC, and once that initial "Oh Crap" shock wears off, then it's back to these basics.

Now that I've "unburied" the lead, and now that we've already talked about educating the attorney who is to defend the CAC, what is left?

Much.

Read the complaint (a/k/a the lawsuit.) See what the allegations (a/k/a claims) are. Try to understand where the Plaintiff's lawyer who has drafted the complaint is coming from. Figure out which parts of the complaint make sense, and which parts of the complaint show a misunderstanding of CACs, of what forensic interviewers do, and also a misunderstanding of the underlying facts that led to the lawsuit.

CAC personnel will more easily be able to evaluate the factual allegations, obviously, then the legal allegations. The legal allegations can range from being fairly straight-forward (such as simple negligence claims) to downright befuddling (such as federal constitutional rights claims). It is important to try your best to understand these federal claims, because you will be armed with factual information that can be used to defeat such claims.

And so the first step in trying to understand these complicated legal claims is to ask. Ask the lawyer to explain, for example, what is meant by the allegation that "negligence" occurred in this particular factual setting, and what are the elements of negligence. If a claim is that the CAC "negligently supervised" a particular employee, likewise have a discussion with the CAC's attorney to discuss the several legal elements of a negligent supervision claim.

And if the claim is that the Plaintiff's federal constitutional rights were violated (known as a §1983 claim), then be prepared for a very long question and answer session. However, it is worth the time and effort, and it is theorized by me that the CAC attorney defending the CAC will think so, too.

One last tip, for now. Follow your attorney's instructions. If there is a request for information, then morph into a hotel *concierge* and comply with all reasonable requests. A lawsuit takes time to wind through the system—it can take more than a year to reach trial—so rest assured you will not be called upon to provide information or be a *concierge* all too often. Besides, be *thankful* you are being asked to work! That means your CAC's attorney is working, too.

In any event, there will probably be much up-front communication because the CAC attorney defending the claim will have to hit the ground running. But after a period of time, and throughout the discovery period, it will become less. That's important to know—you have other pressing and important matters to attend to in your professional lives.

Chapter Nineteen

Laying the Foundation Before Credibility Attacks at Trial

<u>Case:</u> Anderson v. State, Georgia Court of Appeals, Case No.: A11A0306, (Decided April, 2012).

<u>Facts</u>: The Defendant was convicted of three counts of aggravated molestation of his adopted daughter. He married the victim's mother when the victim was very small. The Defendant then moved out of the home in May 2007, when the victim was 9.

Three months earlier, the victim made her first outcry of sexual abuse against Defendant, but when interviewed by law enforcement she recanted. She testified at trial that her recantation was a lie to keep the family together, and that the Defendant "played the guilt trip on her."

Later in 2007, the abuse continued, at the Defendant's apartment. In October 2008, the victim made an outcry to her mother because she was "sick and tired" of the abuse. The next morning, her mother took her to the sheriff's office where an investigator interviewed her. It was recorded and played for the jury. The interview graphically described the abuse. This appeal followed.

A jury charge is an instruction given by the trial judge to jurors that explains the concepts of law that apply to the particular case that the jurors must decide.

Jury charges are critically important. The judge, sitting over the case (and usually above everyone else in the courtroom) is telling the jurors what law applies to the case, and how they are to interpret and apply the charged law in their decision-making process.

It can be very instructive for trial lawyers, when preparing their witnesses for trial, to discuss the standard jury charges that judges use to instruct jurors on the concept of credibility. In my estimation, a conversation with witnesses about credibility in the trial process cannot be done too often.

A standard jury charge on credibility that a judge will provide to the jurors is as follows: "The jury must determine the credibility or the believability of the witnesses.

Therefore, you determine what witness or witnesses you will believe and those which you will not believe, if there are some you do not believe."

The judge then provides the jurors with the facts and circumstances that the jurors can consider when determining credibility. Some include: the witness's manner of testifying; the means and opportunity for knowing the facts that they testify about; the probability or improbability of their testimony; and their interest or lack of interest in the case.

Also, **prior** to the first witness being sworn, the judge will give preliminary instructions, including the credibility instruction. The jurors, if they follow the judge's instructions, use these preliminary charges, in some respects anyway, as a prism through which to view the case.

The power and importance of the jurors' role can be seen from the fact that they alone decide who to believe, and who not to believe.

We care. We care because each of us individually wants to be credible.

We also care because we understand that for justice to be true, other witnesses in the case must be credible, too.

And know this: The credibility of witnesses at trial—yours and others—will depend on the credibility of your work, your standards, and your professionalism prior to trial.

If you are the type of professional on this list who routinely testifies in court because of your professional role, then you are creating a credibility imprint prior to trial when you perform your professional role.

Further, in many aspects of your professional role, you are creating a credibility imprint for other witnesses, many of who often cannot control or manage these credibility concerns on their own. In other words, certain witnesses who might, in fact, be credible still may have to rely on other people to assist them in their credibility needs.

Children, for example.

In this case, an 8-year-old girl disclosed sexual abuse perpetrated on her by her father, and then recanted. Is there anyone who does not believe that this will be a credibility attack at trial on the young girl?

The girl explained the recantation through her own eyes—she lied in her recantation because she wanted the family to stay together and because her father was "guilting" her.

Whether this was enough, standing alone, for the jurors to determine her credibility in her favor we do not know. We do not know because the investigator who interviewed her after her subsequent outcry, which led to the criminal convictions in the case, created a credibility imprint. And the investigator's credibility imprint impacted the investigator's credibility and the victim's credibility in apparently very positive ways.

There are tools and strategies lawyers use to establish credibility at trial. But one of the tools lawyers love to use is the one that shows that work done at the beginning, before the lawyers and the judges and the jurors were involved, was done in a credible and professional manner. In today's case it was—by the investigator who interviewed the victim in 2008 regarding the disclosures at issue in the trial, and which occurred following the recantation.

A defense lawyer might want to test the investigator's confidence in the information that she's receiving from the young child she interviews.

And a SuperWitness investigator understands this—well prior to trial.

In today's case, the investigator took abundantly sufficient steps during the course of her forensic interview to show the jury that the information that she received from the victim was reliable. Not only was this important to the jurors as they returned their guilty verdict, but it was also relied upon by the appellate court in affirming the convictions.

To illustrate the significance of what the investigator did to establish this credibility imprint, I will set out the appellate court's analysis of the investigator's groundwork laid at the beginning of the forensic interview in detail. See what persuades a jury, and an appellate court:

> "Here, Perry (the name of the investigator) testified that the interview took place in a 'children friendly' room at the sheriff's office, outside the presence of J.A.'s (initials of the victim) mother, thus avoiding any undue influence . . . [T]he interview resulted from J.A.'s spontaneous outcry to her mother the day before; and there was no evidence of coercion or coaching. The most recent episode of abuse had taken place only "two or three" weeks before the interview. Perry testified that at first J.A. seemed nervous, but later she was 'very detailed.' J.A. appeared to understand Perry's questions, and her responses to Perry's questions seemed unrehearsed and spontaneous . . . J.A. did not appear to be in any physical or emotional distress; there was no evidence J.A. received either threats or promises; and, to Perry's experienced eye, J.A. did not appear to be under the influence of drugs or alcohol. Perry further testified that, prior to the interview, she had spoken with J.A.'s mother; and that J.A.'s statements in the interview were consistent with the statements J.A. had made to her mother."

Chapter Twenty

The "Victim-Witness" Professional: A Case Study in Getting Subpoenaed When You Don't Expect It

Legal Eagles—Today's case is important because it describes the testimony of a professional who is rarely described in Georgia appellate opinions—the "victim-witness" professional.

Victim-witness professionals have extremely difficult jobs. They are in the front lines of working with the victims and the non-offending caregivers, assisting them in navigating through what can be seen by laypeople as a very complicated, very confusing system. And at the same time, victim-witness professionals are working with families who are in shock, who are upset, who are hurting, and who want answers. Because of their roles, it is probably not at the forefront of their thoughts that they may be called to testify in a child molestation case.

Usually, the appellate decisions related to child molestation cases involve the testimony of such professionals as law enforcement officers, forensic interviewers and evaluators, healthcare professionals and counselors. But it is important for all CACs to understand that an attorney can subpoena any witness who she believes might have relevant information for her case.

This case involves the Defendant's argument on appeal that the victim-witness advocate testified improperly that, according to the defendant on appeal, amounted to testimony that was "overly dramatic" and "intended solely to appeal to the emotions of the jury."

Case: Woods v. State, Georgia Court of Appeals, Case No. A10A1198, (Decided June 11, 2010).

Facts: The Defendant was convicted of three counts of aggravated child molestation, two counts of aggravated battery, and six counts of child molestation related to sexual abuse of his friend's 9-year-old daughter. The abuse occurred over an approximately 6-month period, in the child's home, in isolated areas of parks, and two motels. The Defendant told the victim not to tell. Ultimately, she told her mother, who called the police.

An investigator arranged for a forensic interview at the children's advocacy center, and a sexual abuse examination was performed at a hospital. The victim was able to describe much of the events, some of which she described over time during the investigation. She was able to identify the two hotels, including a hotel registration worker who checked the Defendant and the victim into a room.

The Court of Appeals decision described numerous evidentiary pieces introduced by the prosecution, which resulted in the jury's decision of guilt. Included in the evidence was the testimony of the victim-witness advocate.

The advocate testified that she assisted the victim and her family prior to trial. She testified that she tried to help them get comfortable with the judicial process and the courtroom, for example. During her interaction, she testified that she sat with the victim on four or five occasions with the prosecutor, and during these times she heard the victim disclose details of sexual abuse by the Defendant.

During her testimony, the advocate testified—without objection by the defense lawyer—that she had "dealt with a lot of sexual abuse cases, and I just remember feeling with this one [in] particular that there wasn't anything that . . . he had not done to this child."

During cross-examination, the defense lawyer asked how it was that the advocate was able to recall individual child victims and the specifics of what they said when she did not take any notes during the sessions. After all, the defense was trying to prove, the advocate had been employed as such for 2 ½ years and had worked with at least eight other child victims, meeting with each of them at least three times.

The advocate responded that it was because of her "training and years of experience," and that "each case is different to me."

On re-direct examination, the prosecutor followed up on the defense lawyer's cross-examination, asking: "Why does this case, this particular case, stand out in your mind."

The answer, which was not objected to, was: "Because it was horrific. Because it was one sexual act after another. It was one betrayal of trust after another. And there are some cases that are so horrendous in the level of trust that's been abused and the sexual acts that happen that it stays with you, and this one has stayed with me."

Result: Conviction affirmed.

Good Rules to Know: We'll take the advocate's testimony in chronological order:

1) **Direct Examination**—"I just remember feeling with this one [in] particular that there wasn't anything that . . . he had not done to this child."
2) **Cross Examination**—Because of her "training and years of experience," and that "each case is different to me."

3) **Redirect Examination**—"Because it was horrific. Because it was one sexual act after another. It was one betrayal of trust after another. And there are some cases that are so horrendous in the level of trust that's been abused and the sexual acts that happen that it stays with you, and this one has stayed with me."

The **direct examination** testimony appears to have been made without the prosecutor asking about it. And that makes sense, because the general rule as we know is that the witness cannot testify as to the ultimate issue to be decided by the jury. Thus, the prosecutor is not going to elicit testimony from a witness that invades the jury's role, and which the prosecutor knows is an improper question that could lead to a mistrial

Yet, the statement by the advocate was made, and inexplicably the defense lawyer did not object and then move for a mistrial. The attorney's reason at the Defendant's Motion for New Trial hearing was that she "could not specifically recall why she did not object to this testimony at trial," but she also testified that "the defense's strategy was to attack the credibility of the advocate by showing that (the advocate) had handled many child sexual abuse cases without taking notes on them, yet was somehow able to recall the facts of this case off the top of her head."

The Court of Appeals did not address whether this strategy by the defense attorney was deficient, because it stated that the evidence was overwhelming and it was not reasonably likely that the outcome of the trial would have been different if the defense lawyer had objected to the testimony, or moved for a mistrial.

The **cross examination** testimony was also damaging to the Defendant by the advocate. The defense attorney's stated strategy is a sure-fire loser against people who dedicate their professional lives to assist children who allege abuse, and who are also prepared for trial.

Why wouldn't someone in this field remember horrific abuse allegations that led to one Defendant being charged with 11 counts of molestation charges against one 9-year old girl? Why wouldn't someone who interacts with such a child and who is prepared to testify be able to express this information in vivid and memorable fashion?

So the rule here is that when a softball question is served up, you hit it out of the park. The question, "How can you remember the specifics of this case when you didn't take notes and you have so many cases?" is a softball.

The prosecutor picked up on this very well in **redirect examination.** The prosecutor realized that the defense lawyer opened the door with the defense lawyer's brutally bad strategy. That means that the prosecutor could follow up on redirect examination with this particular thread of testimony, and not have to worry about an objection by the defense lawyer.

And the prosecutor did follow up, giving the advocate free rein to describe why this case, among all of the others, was so memorable to her.

The moral to this story for witnesses regarding the **cross examination** part of this case and the **redirect examination** part of this case is to pause a second or two before answering when you think that the question on the table for you to answer, might be objectionable. Wait to see whether anyone objects. If not, answer the question.

The moral to this story for witnesses regarding the **direct examination** part of the case is, prior to trial, make sure you understand the nature and extent of your testimony that is admissible and proper testimony at trial, especially if you have any concerns that part of your testimony might not be allowed by the rules of evidence.

Chapter Twenty-One

The Dynamics of the Witness Veracity Attack: One Case Study

Legal Eagles—We know about the common defense tactic in child molestation cases to attack the child's veracity. In reading case after appellate case, you can see that the veracity attacks can be broad and across the board: equivocal disclosures; inconsistent statements; wanting to stay in a home; wanting to leave a home; child is too young to believe; child is too old to believe; friends and family members wouldn't believe child under oath; child had a motive to lie.

Good prosecutors and good plaintiff lawyers in civil cases need to understand the rules of evidence that can address these attacks. But also importantly for you, the SuperWitnesses, you need to understand the expert rules of testifying and what an expert can say—and can't say—in light of these veracity attacks.

In this chapter, I have two cases to compare, including a Georgia Court of Appeals case from 2006 that highlighted expert testimony in light of defense veracity attacks. These are good case studies to review and try to make some sense of how an expert can safely testify at trial in this context—and where an expert (or more accurately the lawyer asking her the questions) can run into problems.

Remember that the following is Georgia law, which may or may not be similar to the laws of your state. However, the qualified and competent lawyer of your organization's choosing can easily research the law in your jurisdiction.

Cases:
Hughes v. State, Georgia Court of Appeals, Case No. A0A1925
(decided February 10, 2010).

Patterson v. State, Georgia Court of Appeals
[cite: 278 Ga. App. 168, 628 S.E.2d 618 (2006)]

Facts: In each case, the Defendant was convicted of child molestation charges, and in both cases the victim's veracity was heavily attacked. In the Patterson case, the State's expert was qualified as an expert in both clinical psychology and forensic interviewing. On direct examination, the expert was asked:

> "And at any time did you ever feel like [the victim] made up the story that she told you to get back at her father?" The expert answered, "No."

On cross-examination, the expert acknowledged that she did not have knowledge of certain facts that would indicate that the victim had been disciplined by the defendant-father, and therefore she may have wanted to retaliate against him by making up molestation claims.

On redirect examination, the expert was asked if she believed that the victim had made up the allegations against the defendant "for any reason." In response, the expert said, "No." The Defendant objected to this testimony, claiming that it improperly bolstered the child's credibility.

However, the trial court allowed the expert's testimony on redirect examination because the trial court found that the testimony was admissible to rehabilitate the victim's credibility. This ruling by the trial court was appealed by the Defendant after his conviction.

Result in Patterson: The Court of Appeals reversed the Defendant's conviction and ordered a new trial, because it held that the expert's testimony on redirect examination improperly bolstered the credibility of the victim. Thus, the Court of Appeals found that there is no exception to allow such expert testimony when the victim's veracity is attacked.

The Court of Appeals stated that it will not allow an expert "to give an opinion on a witness's credibility or to express an opinion on the ultimate issue of the defendant's guilt for the purpose of rehabilitating the credibility of another witness whose veracity has been attacked . . . [a] witness, even an expert, can never bolster the credibility of another witness as to whether the witness is telling the truth."

Rationale for rule: Before moving to the Hughes case, it is important to understand why the Georgia courts (and likely your state) has such a rule. In bullet form:

- Given an expert's knowledge and training, testimony that the expert believes the victim is particularly compelling to jurors. Since jurors are the ones charged with determining credibility issues, the courts have consistently held that experts cannot testify regarding truthfulness or credibility of a witness, including the alleged victims.

- Courts recognize that expert testimony may be given increased and particular weight when the credibility of witnesses is a key issue in a case.

- Allowing such testimony would be prejudicial to defendants because of the difficult trial strategy situation they would face, i.e., by challenging the veracity of the victim, they would be opening the door to the State's experts testifying that the victim is telling the truth.

Thus, even in the face of veracity attacks by the Defendant, including testimony by people who swear that they would not believe the victim under oath, the State cannot introduce the testimony of an expert who states that she believes the victim was telling the truth.

Is there no answer to veracity attacks?

In Hughes v. State, the Defendant was convicted of aggravated child molestation involving a 4-year-old victim after a trial that included 10 witnesses, five for the prosecution and five for the defense. According to the Court of Appeals opinion, "[T]he closing arguments turned heavily on the issue of witness credibility."

During trial, the defense lawyer's theory was that the 4-year-old victim had a motive to lie in order to be removed from a foster home. During closing argument, the defense lawyer pointed out that the victim's Sunday school teacher, her pre-K teacher and a Y.M.C.A. employee all testified that they would not believe the victim under oath. He also challenged the credibility of the State's expert.

But it was certain portions of the expert testimony that helped to answer, at least to a degree, the veracity attacks.

During direct examination, the prosecutor asked the State's expert: "Is it unusual for children four years of age to make up allegations of sexual abuse?"

The defense objected, arguing that it went to the ultimate issue in the case. The trial court overruled the objection, stating, "That's not the question. This is a general question, not (a question) about the alleged victim in the case."

The expert then answered. (1) Based on her training and experience, it would be unusual for a child to make up such allegations; and (2) The expert cited a study showing that less than 2 percent of children in the 3—to 6-year-old range made up allegations of abuse.

The Court of Appeals ruled that this testimony was entirely proper, because it goes to issues "beyond the ken of the average juror" and is therefore admissible "even if it indirectly comments on the victim's credibility."

This may seem to be a subtle distinction, but it makes sense. How would the average juror have information related to studies examining the allegations made and reported in a statistically significant survey of child-victims? Further, this specialized knowledge of the expert involves her familiarity with a study of the **general** population, and thus it is not a **direct** comment on this particular victim, even if it is an **indirect comment** of the particular alleged victim in the case.

The Court of Appeals noted that "Such testimony may include a psychologist's evidence that a person with the victim's level of intelligence would have difficulty fabricating a detailed fictional account of abuse, that a child of the victim's age would have difficulty making up a story of abuse, or that a mentally ill victim was capable of distinguishing fact from fiction."

These distinctions in expert testimony are so important to understand, and can be of huge significance at trial. Remember to understand the distinction between information related to children who are part of the general population **(admissible if it is relevant to the issues related to the trial)**, and information that speaks directly to the veracity of this child involved in this trial **(inadmissible if the jury can reach its own conclusion without the help of expert testimony, which is the usual case).**

One last note. In the Hughes case, the prosecutor also asked questions of the expert that went directly to the actual victim's veracity.

Q: "(Did the victim have) the sophistication necessary to make up a lie to . . . get from one home to another.?"

The defense lawyer failed to object, and the expert answered, "I would find that pretty farfetched."

The Court of Appeals in the Hughes case observed that this question "strayed into the area of the personal ability of the victim herself to fabricate allegations with questions that were arguably improper" according to the Patterson v. State case. But, the Court of Appeals stated, the defense lawyer failed to stand up and object to the question at trial, and therefore failed to preserve this issue for the appeal.

So what is the rule for the SuperWitness when getting such a question? Pause—*one thousand one, one thousand two*—and if you hear no objection, then answer the question truthfully and honestly.

Chapter Twenty-Two

Question at Trial: What is the Purpose of Protocols?

Legal Eagles—You're on the stand and the prosecutor asks, "What is the purpose of having protocols?"

Before answering, you understand that in the courtroom a protocol can either be your friend or your nemesis. Established protocols are going to be easily defined and easily applied, and also easy for a good defense lawyer to understand and apply critically to your work product.

I have written so many times in past Legal Letters that it is important to know the established standards and protocols! But what does that really mean anyway? It's kind of like saying eat your vegetables! which when standing alone (as all parents of small children know) may not be such a satisfying statement, let alone a persuasive one.

This topic of protocols can be compared to understanding statutes (a/k/a laws passed by your state's legislature). When I read a statute, I also want to understand the public policy behind it, including the purpose for which our legislators passed it in the first place. When a lawyer understands the public policy behind a statute that has application to a particular case, then she can, by the use of relevant analogies, bring in other statutes or public policies that are helpful to winning the case.

The same with witnesses who have standards and protocols that are specific to their professions. Once they truly understand the purpose of protocols, then the groundwork is laid for performing their jobs responsibly and credibly, and with consistency. It need not be dwelled upon too long that this translates well to the witness stand.

Of course, the inverse is true. Without understanding the protocols and the purpose behind these protocols, a person is very capable of being overwhelmed and impeached on the witness stand, in a very dispiriting way.

When preparing a witness who must follow standards and protocols for trial, the lawyer can go through checklists. With protocols, there can be general checklists and specific checklists. An example of a general checklist, set out below, can be seen as the more universal checklists that have wide application and which can be applied equally to protocols for detectives and to protocols for forensic interviewers.

The Legal Eagles Guide for Children's Advocacy Centers, Part III

On the other hand, specific protocol checklists zero in on a specific profession. That is why a prepared lawyer who preps a witness will interview the witness prior to trial in order to fully understand the specific protocols related to the witness's particular profession.

(As a side note, your state or county may actually have specific protocols in place. Or it may use some national model. You can do some research and find out.)

Many times, the witnesses have not even thought of the purposes—general or specific—behind protocols. That's called failing to see the forest for the trees. I would suggest that once the purposes of protocols can fall off the tip of your tongue, then the work you do in the future cannot help but improve.

The balance of this chapter will discuss protocols in their general sense.

But one more preliminary note: My opinion (which can and will vary from lawyer to lawyer), is that it is more important to describe the reasons behind protocols at trial in their common sense rather than their scientific or technical sense. This is because I know that these protocols as described are going to be provided to jurors, not university professors.

By saying this, I am not suggesting this needs to be expressed in stripped down, elementary forms. But I am suggesting that this discussion should be in terms of basic truths, in the sense that a juror might conclude that they could have application to how a forensic interviewer conducts an interview just as to how an umpire might call balls and strikes.

But be aware! On cross-examination, you may be challenged to recite the scientific and/or technical reasons for protocols. If so, you'll be ready, and be able to define and discuss the protocols in technical terms, before explaining it in plain English. See "How to Be A SuperWitness" chapter, Rule No. 8: "Plain English. Plain English. Plain English. If you have to use professional jargon, say it and then define it in Plain English."

On to protocols:

1. A protocol sets a clear framework from which to work. It is easy to imagine a juror on a child molestation case thinking to himself that the acts and circumstances behind an alleged child molestation, and ultimately the initial disclosure, and then the investigation, and then the collective fallout from all of the above, is a series of chaotic events. An established protocol, on the other hand, is a tried and true method of providing a measured response and measured plan to address these allegations, to commence the investigations, and to assist the affected individuals after a disclosure occurs.

2. An established and reliable protocol, when applied professionally, tends to lead to a reliable result. The strength of this reason is that in the area of child molestation, there are a variety of professionals who follow standards and protocols. Law enforcement has its protocols. Forensic interviewers have theirs.

Forensic evaluators theirs, as do medical professionals and CPS professionals. I am not saying that a lack of any evident protocol, or protocols that are not properly followed, will cause the entire ship to sink. I am saying that protocols that are not understood, are not properly applied, or are simply not followed are prime areas that are ripe for attacks: credibility attacks; attacks on the integrity of the process; and attacks on the organizations and people who respond to allegations of child abuse.

An example is the 2006 case, Tyler v. State, Georgia Court of Appeals (279 Ga. App. 809). There, the Defendant was convicted for child molestation, and appealed because he argued the forensic interview was not conducted according to established standards and protocols. The Defendant also argued that his defense lawyer provided ineffective legal assistance because he did not hire an expert at trial to critique the forensic interview.

Among the "specific protocol" criticisms regarding the forensic interview that were raised on appeal were:

- An improper sequence of questioning;
- The use of repetitive and leading questions;
- The failure to ask follow up questions that would have clarified the alleged ambiguities in the victim's answers; and
- The forensic interviewer, a detective, appeared to have a preconceived bias toward a finding of molestation.

However, the appealed failed and the conviction was affirmed, based upon the Court of Appeals' finding that the defense lawyer had experience in trying child molestation cases, had seen forensic interview tapes before, and cross-examined the detective regarding his forensic interviewing techniques. Thus, according to the Court of Appeals, it could not be demonstrated that the outcome would have been different if the defense had called an expert witness to attack the detective's techniques.

But don't rely on defense attorneys to fail to hire an expert to attack a forensic interviewer's techniques. And don't rely on the legal finding in a random court of appeals opinion that "it could not be demonstrated that the outcome would have been different if the defense had called an expert witness to attack the detective's techniques." Instead, work under the assumption that a forensic interview, or any important work product, can and will be critiqued by someone who is going to be tendered as an expert.

3. An established protocol also provides a clear boundary between your professional responsibilities and those of other MDT members.

One defense attack that stands out when reading the appellate cases involving child molestation trials is the one that suggests a particular professional overstepped the boundaries of his role. At that point, the argument goes, the person's objectivity and quest for the truth ended and his advocacy or bias toward a particular result began.

We have discussed this topic in past chapters. Know your roles. Know how to precisely explain to jurors why you are performing those roles, which while different from other MDT members does not mean that they have to be in conflict. Instead, they are seen as distinct pieces of the puzzle, which cannot be put together when a person such as a forensic interviewer has, as an example, somehow managed to overreach by performing something resembling a therapeutic function. Established "general statements" regarding protocols can assist in establishing these reasonable boundaries.

Clearly there are other general statements to be made regarding protocols. It's worth a healthy discussion at an MDT meeting. Protocols promote reliability. Reliable evidence in the courtroom leads to credibility. Credibility wins cases, and that means justice.

Chapter Twenty-Three

Give Circumstantial Evidence the Respect it Deserves!

Legal Eagles—Circumstantial evidence can carry the day in trials, but what is it really? Do I need to see the rain falling from the sky to testify that it is now raining? No, that's direct evidence which is perfectly good proof.

But what if I'm in my office cubicle with no windows because my boss wants me to work real hard. Just after you walk into my view, I see you stomp your galoshes on the floor, causing puddles, and you shake your umbrella closed as rainwater sprays into my cubicle. I say out loud, without seeing outside, "It's raining outside." That is circumstantial evidence, which also is perfectly good proof.

One key to reliable and credible circumstantial evidence is to be able to pile layer upon layer of credible facts that build this circumstantial evidence monster. This can be seen by how our appellate courts review cases that are determined on the strength of circumstantial evidence. In child molestation cases, it goes without saying the circumstantial evidence is critical and cannot be overlooked by prosecutors. But it is also a topic that professionals who will be called as witnesses—expert and otherwise—need to thoroughly understand, as today's case will make clear.

Case: Viers v. State, Georgia Court of Appeals, Case No. A09A2293, (Decided March 8, 2010).

Facts: The Defendant was convicted of aggravated child cruelty and cruelty to a child after bringing his 2 ½ year old daughter to the ER wrapped in a blanket, and telling medical personnel that his daughter had fallen down steps earlier and was bleeding from her vaginal area. The victim was naked under the blanket, and a bath towel was between her legs. She had grass and twigs in her perineal and groin area, but none in her wet hair. She had multiple bruises on her body, some of which appeared to be old, and some appeared to be fresh. Some of the bruises were in the shape of a hand.

Two medical doctors testified. The first was a surgeon who performed corrective surgery on the victim's perineum. He testified that her injuries were not consistent with a fall, or other traumatic episodes suggested by the defense. He testified that the injuries were consistent with abuse, and that a stick could have caused them. On cross-examination, the doctor testified that the victim's injuries could have been caused "by a significant straddle injury."

The second doctor was a forensic pediatrician who examined the victim the day after her surgery. He testified that he observed lacerations in the victim's anus, and was questioned about the cause of the victim's injury:

> "Did a dog bite cause this? The answer is no. Did a fall down the steps cause this? The answer is no. Did a fall into bushes cause this? I very much doubt it. The possibility remains that this child may have received what is called a straddle injury, where a child falls, and you typically see it on a playground or under a bicycle or something like that, where that area between the genitalia and the anus strikes something hard and can bruise or lacerate the skin. I was not supplied a history that would suggest that a straddle injury had happened, but I cannot rule it out."

The doctor then testified that the victim's injuries were consistent with sexual abuse and insertion of a stick into her anus.

Following conviction, the Defendant appealed on numerous grounds, including the one to be discussed today regarding circumstantial evidence. That is, the Defendant argued that his conviction was based upon circumstantial evidence and that the evidence presented at trial did not rule out the hypothesis that the victim suffered a "straddle injury."

Result: Conviction affirmed.

Good rule to know: In Georgia, the statute (a/k/a law) that lays out the use of circumstantial evidence in criminal trial is O.C.G.A. § 24-4-6. For you out-of-Georgia Legal Eagles, you know where I'm going with this—consult the qualified legal representative of your choice who will easily be able to locate your state's equivalent statue or legal rule.

> "To warrant a conviction on circumstantial evidence, the proved facts shall not only be consistent with the hypothesis of guilt, <u>but shall exclude every other reasonable hypothesis</u> save that of the guilt of the accused." (Emphasis mine.)

Just thinking out loud, but every case that doesn't involve eyewitnesses to the alleged molestation (other than the alleged perpetrator and the alleged victim) has the distinct probability of involving a defense that will raise alternative hypotheses suggesting innocence. Understand this. Anticipate this. At the risk of being repetitive, review the forensic pediatrician's trial testimony once more:

> "Did a dog bite cause this? The answer is no. Did a fall down the steps cause this? The answer is no. Did a fall into bushes cause this? I very much doubt it. The possibility remains that this child may have received what is called a straddle injury, where a child falls, and you typically see it on a playground or under a bicycle or something like that, where that area between the genitalia and the anus strikes something hard and can bruise or lacerate the skin. I was not supplied a history that would suggest that a straddle injury had happened, but I cannot rule it out."

A confidence in his knowledge of his craft, and a keen understanding of the factual elements of the case, made this testimony powerful because there was _no way_ that the defense could proffer any information that the victim suffered a straddle injury.

In fact, this is the second part of the rule related to whether a conviction based on circumstantial evidence is warranted. When the defense in criminal cases "offers an explanation of circumstantial facts or an alternative hypothesis of events, the reasonableness of that explanation is for the factfinder."

In other words, the "factfinder," a/k/a the jurors, are the ones to decide whether the prosecutor's evidence, even though circumstantial, is sufficient to exclude every reasonable hypothesis except that of the Defendant's guilt.

Finally, today's case is instructive in that the Georgia Court of Appeals took the time in its opinion to list all of the pieces of circumstantial evidence that led to its approval of the jury's verdict—more than a dozen. As for the Defendant, the Court of Appeals stated that he "gave multiple conflicting explanations for [the victim's] injuries, none of which were supported by the evidence.

You know defenses of "alternative hypotheses" are inevitable. Collecting the information through professional standards and protocols is a powerful tool for the toolbox.

Chapter Twenty-Four

Discussing Some of the Dynamics that Occur in Child Custody Cases

Legal Eagles—Child custody battles. What do those three words do for you?

Add allegations of one former spouse that the other has sexually abused one of their children, and wants to modify the Court-ordered custody agreement accordingly. Add a vehement denial and aggressive defense by the accused. Add that law enforcement investigated the allegations and determined that the child molestation allegations were unfounded.

The criminal prosecution won't be going forward, but rest assured, there will be litigation in the civil arena in front of a judge who must decide whether to modify a previous order establishing the parameters of who takes care of the child (or children) and when. In this situation, one side is going to argue that there was insufficient evidence to move a criminal investigation forward.

Also, in this situation, a CAC forensic interviewer whose F.I. product was used during the course of the criminal investigation is going to be subpoenaed in the custody case. One might think there will be unique pressures brought to bear on the forensic interviewer by both sides. Stop, and be calm. Professionals, who happen to testify, are going to testify as to the facts and information as it came to them, and call it like they see it. Always.

After that, a judge or a jury is going to make a decision.

This chapter's case is a study in such a decision-maker, the judge in the custody case.

Case: Hardin v. Hardin, Georgia Court of Appeals, Case No. A10A054, (Decided April 6, 2010).

Facts: Following a divorce from her husband, the mother was granted sole custody of their three children, ages 4 ½, 2 and 1. The father was granted visitation rights. The divorce order was entered on February 13th. Shortly after, the 5-year-old and the 2-year-old allegedly told the mother that the father had inappropriately touched them, and on May 23rd, the mother filed petition with the Court to modify custody. (All dates are from 2006.)

Understand what this does, in Georgia. Based upon the allegations, the trial court issued an order suspending the father's visitation until the resolution of the abuse allegations.

A timeline is in order.

- May 9th—Mother reports her children's' disclosures to the County Department of Family and Children Services ("DFCS")

- May 23rd—Mother's petition to modify custody is filed

- May 24th—A pediatrician with extensive training in child sexual abuse examined the children, and found no evidence of sexual abuse, but found that the children's allegations of abuse were credible.

- A psychologist performed a psychological examination on both parents (date not reported in court of appeal's opinion), and determined that the children's allegations were "highly credible."

- Between May 9th and August 28th, DFCS completed its investigation. After a preliminary review, DFCS substantiated the allegations of child abuse. It then went to a panel review, and the department changed its findings to unsubstantiated and closed its file.

- Between May 9th and August 28th, law enforcement completed its investigation. It found the charges were unfounded because the father passed a polygraph test and there was no medical evidence of abuse.

The modification hearing was held August 28th. Both the psychologist and pediatrician testified as above, and the pediatrician testified that in her experience 4-year-olds do not fabricate such events. Evidence was introduced that the father had an "affinity" for pornography, and that he had acted inappropriately toward his 16-year-old stepdaughter. The guardian ad litem, noting the father's "pornographic predilection," recommended that the father's visitation rights not be restored. The father testified, and denied touching the children inappropriately.

The father also testified that he recently married an 18-year-old woman, who was 20 years younger than him, and who had an 18-month old daughter. He testified that he thought his wife was 27 years old when he married her. He testified that she was "somewhere in Tennessee," but had no contact information for her.

First Result: What do you think? How would you decide? You should know that the standard of proof in these kinds of cases in Georgia is the preponderance of the evidence standard, not proof beyond a reasonable doubt as in criminal cases. So, as we civil lawyers like to say, the mother just has to slightly tip those scales of justice ever so slightly in her favor—50.00001% works.

The trial court concluded that the evidence was not "persuasive enough to establish a ruling denying visitation rights" to the father.

Good rule to know: The Court of Appeals is not going to re-weigh the evidence. Weighing the evidence is the function of the judge (in this case) or a jury, in a jury trial. The judge in this case or a jury is there to see and hear the parties, see and hear the witnesses, see and observe demeanor, and attitudes, and assess credibility. Courts of Appeals can't do that by reviewing pages and pages of transcripts.

Further, "where there is any evidence to support the trial court's finding, it cannot be said that the court abused its discretion. As the evidence of sexual abuse was not conclusive, we cannot say that the trial court abused its discretion in denying Mother's petition."

Do I have to again tell you how difficult your jobs are?

One more point, regarding the outcome of this particular case. Following the hearing, but before the trial court entered its order denying the mother's modification request, the mother's lawyer located the father's new wife. The lawyer wrote the Court seeking to re-open the evidence for the Court to consider in the form of supplemental evidence. The Court denied the request, stating that the evidence was closed.

Second Result: The Court of Appeals found that the trial court was in error denying this case, and reversed the trial court's decision on this point and ordered that it consider the additional evidence.

Good Rule to Know #2: "Where the issue is a material change in conditions [such as alleged abuse of a son or daughter] it is error to refuse to hear any evidence which might have some bearing upon that issue. Where the welfare of a child is involved, relevant information must be received up until the very time that the court rules." (Inserted words are mine.)

Chapter Twenty-Five

Evidence That Appellate Judges Rely Upon

<u>Case:</u> Dozier v. State, Georgia Court of Appeals, Case No. A11A1085, (Decided September 19, 2011).

<u>Facts</u>: The Defendant was convicted of rape, aggravated sodomy, aggravated child molestation, child molestation and incest for crimes against his then 14-year-old daughter.

The Defendant did not live with the victim, but would pick her up from school and drive her behind a commercial building and force her to have sex. Other times, he visited her home when her mother was not at home, and abused her.

Testimony at trial regarding the delayed disclosure included evidence that the victim thought the Defendant would physically harm and choke her, and that the Defendant told her that no one would believe her. Further, she testified that she did not want her mother to feel bad or angry with her for not disclosing the abuse sooner.

Eventually, the victim disclosed to her boyfriend, and then her mother learned of the abuse. Her mother immediately took her to the police station.

We've been at this Legal List for about four years now. Most of the time, we discuss the variety of statutes, legal theories and legal rules that directly impact folks who work in or with Children's Advocacy Centers. The import of knowing this information cannot be overstated.

However, as I reflect on these Legal Letters, I realize that I have not written too many times about what facts, information and evidence resonates with appellate judges, who are writing all of these opinions regarding child molestation trials.

There are certain themes when reading appellate opinions that jump out at me. You can start with credibility. And underneath the credibility umbrella you find experience, professionalism, training, and competence.

This week, I read the opinion in Dozier v. State, where the father was convicted for the ongoing abuse of his 14-year-old daughter. The issue on appeal was not necessarily relevant to what you do—the Defendant appealed because he believed that the trial court made an error at trial when the trial court admitted evidence of one of his a prior convictions for impeachment purposes.

But rather than discuss the intricacies of such impeachment evidence, I believe the narrative portion of the appellate judge's opinion will be extremely interesting and I hope very helpful to you in understanding the type of information that appellate judges use in order to support their ultimate decision in the appeals before them.

In today's case, in fact, I thought the appellate judge's summary of the evidence was so well-written and so well-summarized, that I am going to set it out here.

Please take note about how the appellate judge summarizes the evidence and testimony related to each witness who encountered the victim after the victim's outcry. Understand from the summary what information is determined to be credible by this court, and how that information is well within the reach of what you do:

* * *

The victim testified that she did not want Dozier to perform the sexual acts but did not fight back because she was afraid he would "body slam" and choke her. She did not tell anyone about the abuse right away because Dozier said if she did, she would get in trouble and "it all [would] come back on [her]" because no one would believe her. She also did not want to make her mother feel bad or be angry with her for not disclosing the abuse sooner.

The victim finally made an outcry to her boyfriend, who told the victim's cousin. The cousin told her mother, who was the victim's aunt, and the aunt drove the two girls to pick up the victim's mother. In the car on the way back to the aunt's house, the victim told her mother what had been happening with Dozier. The mother was upset but not angry with the victim, and took her to the police station immediately to make a report. Investigation and prosecution ensued.

In addition to the victim, her boyfriend, cousin, and mother all testified about the outcry. An expert in child sexual abuse examinations testified that she had examined the victim, who reported a year-long history of penile-vaginal penetration and oral sex that began the day before her fourteenth birthday. The victim's gynecological examination was essentially normal, which the expert explained did not rule out sexual abuse because the tissue in that area tended to heal quickly.

An expert in forensic interviews of sexually abused children testified that she was the director of the non-profit Georgia Center for Child Advocacy, which works closely with the police and the Department of Family and Children's Services. The center's staff are specially trained to talk to children in a non-leading, non-suggestive way to obtain information when someone suspects that a child has been abused or can provide information about child abuse.

The expert explained that children who are abused by someone within their social or family circle often disclose the abuse more slowly than if the abuser were a stranger. When the abuser is someone in a position of authority in a child's life, the expert said, the child may be used to obeying that person's commands, such as "clean your room" or "eat your supper," and thus obey the command not to tell anyone what is happening to them. Children also commonly fear that no one will believe them, that they are responsible for the abuse, and that they will be punished or be the cause of someone else's punishment if discovered. Sometimes an abused child reveals no outward change in her demeanor, but once the abuse is disclosed the child may reveal more information as time passes and she assesses the reaction to her disclosure.

A detective who works in a special victims' unit for crimes against women and children testified that he watched the forensic interview of the victim to observe her demeanor and to obtain basic background information about the incidents she had disclosed. She was "humble," the detective said, showing neither sorrow nor happiness. The detective interviewed Dozier twice, at Dozier's residence and then at the police station, and the State played recordings of both interviews during trial. The detective testified that he thought it was strange that Dozier remembered small details about a shopping trip with the victim but could not remember whether or not he had driven his car behind the building, where the victim said one of the assaults occurred.

Dozier testified and denied abusing the victim. He also testified on direct examination that he "took a plea bargain" on an aggravated assault charge in 1993 and spent time in prison. During cross-examination, Dozier admitted writing a letter to someone in which he said, "Please help me change her testimony," but said he was referring to his ex-girlfriend, not to the victim.

* * *

You can see how the appellate judge used the involvement of the witnesses to weave the story of the Defendant's abuse. The appellate judge did so by providing the evidence introduced by each witness that supported the jury's determination that the Defendant was guilty. Finally, the appellate judge referred often to the "expertise" of the various witnesses, and you will notice that the information attributed to each of the experts was significant for the matter-of-fact manner in which it was conveyed. Credibility matters, in appeals too!

Chapter Twenty-Six

The Substandard Lawyer Performance— And What You Can Do About It

Legal Eagles—In this chapter, I'd like to discuss a topic that relates to the courtroom work of lawyers that was perceived as being substandard.

It would be great if I could write that lawyers are always going to be prepared for trial by fully understanding the facts of the case, and understanding your science, profession, industry or trade. Or that they will be able to make all of the proper objections, while at the same time protecting you from unfair characterizations on the witness stand by the other party's attorney.

That would be nice if always true, instead of fiction. So how do you address this sticky topic with the attorneys, whether they are prosecutors or any other lawyer who calls you as a witness?

Take it from a lawyer who has lost cases, and who has had the humbling experience of speaking with jurors after a loss. If I can state the three words that these jurors almost always say to the losing lawyer after a case, it would be these: "We just believed . . ."

To the losing lawyer, the "just" in "We just believed . . ." signifies that the jurors did not believe the lawyer, or the lawyer's evidence, or the lawyer's witnesses. All of these are failings of the lawyer and no one else. So when lawyers do poorly at trial, they need to know why.

Deciding when to discuss lawyer malfunction can be tricky. Getting in the lawyer's grill right after trial, or in the day or two following, may be counterproductive whether the lawyer is thick-skinned or not.

My view of "when" is similar to my view of when a witness should start preparing for trial. A witness should start preparing for trial the day she opens the file, or the day a case is assigned, or the day she meets with the client. In other words, a witness should prepare for trial far in advance of the actual court date, when each step in the inevitable but slow march toward a trial date can be properly documented, properly completed, and professionally done.

But more of the "when" later. First, my theory of talking to lawyers about their so-so performances has twin pillars, and each should properly be in place.

93

The first pillar is be careful about jumping into this conversation before you have done your part and have a checked checklist that looks like this:

My CV is updated, is as brief as possible, is professional and packs a punch.

- ✓ I have completed all necessary professional trainings or certifications, or am in the active process of doing so, and continue to complete ongoing trainings in my area.

- ✓ I "own" my professional area, in that I am aware of all of the literature, standards, protocols, journal articles or treatises. I stay informed about my profession on an ongoing basis. I know the criticisms and attacks that are out there, and have carefully reviewed their points of view.

- ✓ I am aware of the legal rules that affect my testimony, such as hearsay, child hearsay, rules related to expert testimony, rules related to the "ultimate issue," witness bolstering, the rule of sequestration, etc.

- ✓ I give back to the community, whether large or small, whether while I am at work or in my own time, in areas related to my professional pursuits. When I am on the witness stand, it will become apparent that I can talk the talk because I walk the walk.

- ✓ When I am first assigned a case, or a file, or a client, I have a standard, habitual routine of opening files and completing paperwork that is so meticulous it makes me look like I trained with the Marines at Parris Island.

- ✓ When I add materials to my file, I do so based upon my skill, training, experience and protocol. When someone looks at my file two years from now it will make sense to him—and me.

- ✓ I understand my role, and I understand my limitations. I am a (detective) (forensic interviewer)(counselor)(child and family advocate)(child protective services professional). My activities will reflect such, and I do not overreach in my role or my responsibilities.

- ✓ When I learn that I am going to be called to testify, I will make sure that I know my file inside out, with no exceptions.

- ✓ When I think of testifying in court, I will welcome the opportunity to tell what I know or what I have seen or what I believe.

And guess what? It's not even an exhaustive checklist! But a checklist like that will put you in a position where you're more prepared than a good number of lawyers ever will be. A checklist like that will allow you to have credibility with the lawyer, and an indication that you are doing—and have done—everything you can to be an effective witness at trial. Ultimately, your good reputation will also speak for you. A conversation between a witness who has done a poor job in preparing and testifying at trial and a lawyer who has done a poor job at trial is a sorry conversation indeed.

That leads to the second pillar, related to "when" to talk to the lawyer. My view is based upon the common-sense "preventative medicine" approach. If I eat healthy, exercise, go to the various doctors on a scheduled and routine basis, then chances are I won't have to put out the medical fires and live in medical crisis.

Trials are that way. What good is it, after all, to walk up to the losing lawyer afterward and tell him what a lousy job he did because he didn't ask you this, or anticipate that, or understand your concerns in these areas? And so we've talked over time in these Legal Letters about the importance of being able to go to the prosecutor or the lawyer calling you as a witness prior to trial when it does the most good and tell her your concerns.

Every witness, even most of those seasoned CAC detectives who've been on the stand countless times, have concerns. So the second pillar, after you've established the first, is to be able to discuss with the subpoenaing lawyer your concerns prior to trial.

As part of this, you can learn what the lawyer is intending to show or prove with your testimony. As part of this, you can discuss the likely topics that will be raised by the other lawyer. As part of this, you can inform the lawyer who subpoenas you the manner in which you're most comfortable explaining the information that you're going to testify about. As part of this, you can inform the lawyer what you don't know or what you haven't done as part of your involvement in the case.

And finally, as part of this you can discuss the wild card topic that is on your mind. These relate to the times you've been on the witness stand in the past and had bad experiences, some of which were because the lawyer who brought you was not fully prepared. These, I believe, are the times to discuss your concerns and even your constructive criticisms, before the trial when they can be addressed. It takes being proactive on your part, but it allows you to go into your testimony with your eyes wide open. Good luck!

Epilogue and Acknowledgments

I wrote it at the beginning of the book: My vision for every CAC in the United States is to have access to competent and reliable legal counsel. That vision is far removed from where we are in 2012. My belief is that the vast majority of CACs in the country do not. Think about that for a minute.

It is inevitable that a CAC's involvement with children who are suspected victims of child abuse, will involve legal matters. A thorough understanding of the myriad legal issues that can and routinely do arise, and that affect CACs, cannot be fully understood and appreciated by lay people. This is why we need to strive to have uniform legal council for all CACs in the United States.

CACs have multidisciplinary team members. Law enforcement has legal counsel. Medical has legal counsel. Child protective services have legal counsel. If there is an education piece on the MDT, it has legal counsel. The prosecutor's office obviously has legal counsel.

What is missing? The one entity that organizes the whole show. The one entity that regularly houses the records. The one entity whose professionals routinely testify.

Just look at all of the things that legal council could do: Ensure all CACs have updates to relevant statues and case law; give immediate email blasts with "breaking news" with follow ups; obtain transcripts of relevant court testimony, summarized, and provided to CACs for courtroom testimony preparation; file appellate briefs as friends of the court in cases appeals where CAC interests are affected; network with all other state CAC organizations, as well as national organizations such as NCA and NCAC, to share best practice data; update, on nationwide scale, all laws, appellate decisions, research and trends affecting CACs; maintain "core" studies and research that is routinely cited in court by attorneys and others.

And of course, work on behalf of the CAC itself in all of the legal areas that need to be addressed, in a manner that looks after the best interest of the CAC itself.

Properly responding to legal matters should be seen as a large part of advocacy for children. In fact, a CAC will be held accountable by judges and lawyers in the courtroom to being responsibly and professionally represented when it responds to legal matters that affect it.

Legal counsel for CACs should be standard. I provide a full day, packed to the rafters, workshop titled "Law and CACs" that will provide CACs with an eye-opening overview of the importance of legal counsel. The goal of the program is to help the CAC establish legal counsel as one of its standards. In fact, the standard is this: "The Children's Advocacy Center will have reliable, effective, and competent legal representation to meet all its legal responsibilities."

With that, I thank you. Thank you to the CAC center directors, forensic interviewers, forensic evaluators, child and family advocates, child protective service workers, law enforcement officials, medical personnel, private practice counselors, law professors, and others who have the time to join the List Serv, read the weekly Legal Letters, and provide invaluable feedback. I am still the "behind the scenes" guy who is trying to lend a hand to you who are at the forefront with a career that is essential, needed and noble.

I also thank my wonderful legal assistant Ivana Alic' who tirelessly worked on this project. I am very grateful to her for her work, but especially her interest in this important topic.

I can be reached through my website www.AgatstonLaw.com. Please contact me if you would like to be added to the weekly Legal List, a free service for CAC Legal Eagles. If I can assist in trainings for your Center or your state's CAC Network, I am ready, willing and able. Best regards!

www.ingramcontent.com/pod-product-compliance
Lightning Source LLC
Chambersburg PA
CBHW030908180526
45163CB00004B/1751